THOUGHTS *of an* UNLIKELY MESSENGER

Copyright © 2015 by Carl Burton

Cover and interior design by Masha Shubin

Cover Images: Apocalypse After War © Udra11 (DreamsTime.com); All-seeing-eye Pyramid Symbol © Microvector (BigStockPhoto.com).

All Bible verses are King James Version.

All rights reserved. No part of this book may be reproduced or transmitted in any form or by any means whatsoever, including photocopying, recording or by any information storage and retrieval system, without written permission from the publisher and/or author. The views and opinions expressed in this book are those of the author(s) and do not necessarily reflect those of the publisher, and the publisher hereby disclaims any responsibility for them. Neither is the publisher responsible for the content or accuracy of the information provided in this document. Contact Inkwater Press at inkwater.com. 503.968.6777

    Burton, Carl, 1983- author.
       Thoughts of an unlikely messenger / by Carl Burton.
    pages cm
    LCCN 2015936831
    ISBN 978-1-62901-236-0 (pbk.)
    ISBN 978-1-62901-237-7 (Kindle ebk.)
    ISBN 978-1-62901-238-4 (ePub)
    ISBN 978-1-62901-264-3 (hc)

    1. Burton, Carl, 1983- 2. Christian biography--United States. 3. Bible--Criticism, interpretation, etc. 4. Conspiracy theories. 5. History--Miscellanea. 6. Autobiographies. I. Title.

BR1725.B87A3 2015   277.308'3092
                           QBI15-1403

Publisher: Inkwater Press | www.inkwaterpress.com

Paperback ISBN-13 978-1-62901-236-0 | ISBN-10 1-62901-236-X
Hardback ISBN-13 978-1-62901-264-3 | ISBN-10 1-62901-264-5
Kindle   ISBN-13 978-1-62901-237-7 | ISBN-10 1-62901-237-8
ePub   ISBN-13 978-1-62901-238-4 | ISBN-10 1-62901-238-6

Printed in the U.S.A.

3 5 7 9 10 8 6 4 2

THOUGHTS
of an
Unlikely Messenger

CARL BURTON

PORTLAND • OREGON
INKWATERPRESS.COM

TABLE OF CONTENTS

Chapter 1: Teaching the Innocent to Sin 1
Chapter 2: Doing What I Felt I Had To 12
Chapter 3: My Secret and the Meaning 32
Chapter 4: Free Love 52
Chapter 5: The Beginning of the End 68
Chapter 6: An Organized Plan 86
Chapter 7: Testimony of the True Church 111
Chapter 8: Wars and Rumors of Wars 135
Chapter 9: The Time of Purification 152
Chapter 10: The Fall 166
Chapter 11: The Wrath of God 191

CHAPTER 1

TEACHING THE INNOCENT TO SIN

August 18, 1983, in Detroit, Michigan, I was born at Holy Cross Hospital. Born an innocent child of light, but as time passed and I grew older, I began to slowly indulge in the darkness of sin, blinded by the ways of the world. I always hear people say, "We are all born into sin." I don't believe a child is born a sinner, but I definitely know and believe a person can be raised into one. I want to tell you a little bit about my life, because I am a firm believer that to understand the present and to see where a person is going, you have to understand where a person has been.

I grew up on the west side of Detroit, but it doesn't really matter what side of town you stay on; it's all the ghetto. I was raised by my mother, and being a single mother with four boys, it wasn't always an easy task, but she always did the best she could. I guess my job as a brother was a little bit harder, me being the oldest and all. I had to try to be a good role model to my little brothers. I think that I did an okay job of that growing up. I have a sister on my father's side of the family, who I really only got to see at funerals growing up. I was so happy to see her at a barbeque a few years back, because for a moment, I had forgotten what she even looked like. My grandparents were always around, helping, teaching, and guiding us to make sure we stayed out of trouble. Especially since all the men my mother fell for could never stay out of jail. My father was never really around while I was growing up, because he was always running the streets. I found out that my father was in the streets, because after he was murdered, I tried to get Social Security. They told me my father only had one real job in his life, at a moving company he worked at for a little over three months. I didn't really know what type of man he was; I only had a few memories of him growing up. I learned more about my father after his death from stories from family members than when he was alive.

I looked at my grandfather as the male role model and influence in my life. As a child I spent most of my time with my grandfather, who taught me just about everything. It is through his wisdom and teachings that I am who I am today. I guess the bond with me and my father was broken, because I never really liked going to his house as a child. They had mice and roaches; not just night roaches either, but the kind that came out whenever they felt like it. I didn't want to eat anything that didn't come straight off of the stove, because they would crawl on the table, and sometimes I caught them on the food if it had been sitting out for too long. Night times were the worst, though, because there were so many people that stayed in the house. I knew they would make me sleep on the floor. It's not that I didn't love that side of the family, but I could never get a good night's sleep knowing that there was a chance something could crawl on me or bite me while I was asleep. The other reason I never wanted to go over there was because I wet the bed until I was eleven. It was so embarrassing, and it wasn't exactly easy to cover up the fact you wet the floor. The whole room smelled like piss, but I couldn't help it; I had a weak bladder. I can only remember seeing my father about five times in my life. It seemed the older I got, the further we moved apart. One thing I can remember we always did was play basketball with the crate we hooked up to the gate in the backyard of his house. Those were moments with my father that I will always cherish and remember forever.

When my father and my mother split up, I was still a toddler. After their breakup, she met a guy named Keith. Keith was the reason I bought my first pack of cigarettes when I was five. Keith was hooked on drugs, and he used to send me and my three-year-old brother to the gas station on the corner to get his cigarettes. We thought the cigarettes made him act crazy, which was why we begged our mother to quit smoking them. Now that I am older and I think back, I realize he was addicted to crack. I remember he was high one day and put my younger brother in the shower with just the hot water on and aimed it at his feet as a punishment. He ended up with third-degree burns on his feet. I was afraid to tell my mother what really happened. He threatened to get me next if I said anything to her. I still don't think she knows what happened to this day, but my mother always stood by her man, no matter what happened. Sometimes I even felt like she picked them over me. I think that, in a way, she knew he was hooked on drugs the whole time. She just didn't want to believe that the man she was with was hooked on them. It came out, though, because Keith had stolen a few things out of the house and sold them for crack. When my mother noticed things missing, she put him out of the house. She didn't want him around us anymore, but Keith couldn't let go, and he tried to come back. They got into a big argument and he threw hot grease on my mother while she was holding my infant brother. After that, she took out a restraining order on him, and he spent a little time in jail. I was about six when it happened, but I remember that like it was yesterday.

    Growing up, I have always felt different, like I never really fit in anywhere. I used to want to be like everybody else, sometimes I still do, but every time I've tried, it has brought me nothing but trouble. Still, sometimes it just felt better to fit in than to feel alone. I guess that's why when I was growing up I got into so many fights. Even though I felt different, I never liked being treated like I was different. So at times, I did whatever I could to fit in with the people around me. I guess when you're young you don't realize that being your own person and being different is God's gift to you, so why hide it? It's not until you truly embrace who you are that you can be truly happy. I got into most of my fights in school, but sometimes I got into fights with the neighborhood kids. I guess you could say I had a bad temper, because a person could do or say the slightest thing to me to trigger the fight. It wasn't until the seventh grade that all the fighting caught up with me. I was kicked out of all Detroit Public Schools for the rest of the year for fighting. I don't even remember what started the fight, but after the fight, I sat in the office terrified. I didn't know how my mother or my grandparents were going to take the fact that I got put out of all Detroit Public Schools. All I remember is that my mother left work early to come get me. I had to have an adult come get me off school grounds. When my mother got there, she begged the school to give me another chance. She assured the principal that it wouldn't happen again. After they told her there was nothing they could do for me, we got in the car and left. I knew something was wrong; I could feel it in my gut. The ride home was the scariest part, because we went home, straight home, in silence, no music and no talking. She didn't even turn to look at me once while she was driving. I thought about jumping out of the car while it was moving and taking my chances, but by the time I worked up enough courage to do it, we were in the driveway.

When we made it home, she told me to come to the basement. She disciplined me and it was the worst beating I ever had in my life. It was the only one I could never forget. Not only because of the pain, but because it was the moment that changed my life. After she got tired and decided she was done, I thought about it. I was confused as to why I got punished for something I got taught to do, defend myself. After all, she was the one who taught me never to let anyone pick on me and to win every fight by any means necessary. I could tell it was about more than just fighting, because when I looked at her face, she was crying hysterically. I thought about how hard it must be for her to raise four boys by herself. Even though my mother was a kind, church-going woman, every man that came into her life never seemed to be any good. My father was a hustler, Keith got hooked on drugs, and Thomas was always doing something illegal, so he couldn't stay out of jail. She played two roles in the house, one as my mother and the other as my father. As she was crying, she turned to me and told me she loved me. She reached out to give me a hug, but her wrapping her arms around me only caused more pain, because I was still sore from her actions. Then she looked me right in the eyes and told me she was sorry. She explained to me that she didn't know what else to do and she begged me to stop. She was afraid the road I was going down would either lead me to jail or to an early grave. Since she had seen all the men she loved go to jail, maybe she saw a little bit of them in me. Seeing her cry like that was one of the most painful things I ever had to look at. I promised her after that day I was going to do better and try to stop fighting, that I was going to go to school and make something of myself, and that one day she would be proud of me.

I ended my time at Detroit Public Schools, and I started my new school that next week. It was a charter school on the border of Detroit, right outside of the city in the suburbs. I thought maybe I could get a fresh start in a new school. Nobody knew me there, so nobody expected anything from me. I tried my best to keep my promise to my mother, Lord knows I tried. It seemed as though the harder I tried to stay out of trouble, the more trouble found me. At my new school, I quickly found out that being a class clown had more benefits than a trip to the office or detention. I got into another fight, and I felt so bad after the fight, because I had broken my promise. I know I told myself I wouldn't fight anymore, but my pride wouldn't let me back down from this one. I tried to think of ways to avoid being in fights, especially since my grandfather had got involved afterward and he threaten to embarrass me in front of the class if I had one more incident. I tried not being the class clown and it worked for a while. That is, until we got a new student in our homeroom class. He sat right behind me in a few classes and right next to me in art. He turned out to be sort of a bully in the sense that he was aggravating, annoying and always doing something behind my back. It was almost like he knew I couldn't fight back. I don't have any idea what I did, but he chose me to pick on. I remembered what my mother said, and I tried everything to avoid him. I even tried not sitting near him at our table in the lunchroom. I asked all my teachers if I could change my seats in my classes. I even went out a different door at the end of the day. All so I wouldn't get embarrassed in front of my friends. Then one day in art class, he started breaking crayons and throwing them across the room trying to hit me. One of the crayons hit me in the face and the class busted out laughing at me. The pressure was on and I had to do something or else everybody would have started doing it. In my mind, that was the last draw. I couldn't look like the coward, and he had embarrassed me in front of everybody. So I had to make a choice of which was worse, being embarrassed by your grandfather or one of your classmates. I stood up walked over to where he was sitting and punched him until I could barely move my hand. After the fight was over, they took me to the hospital for my hand. Even though I was in pain, I felt great. I had regained my dignity and respect from my classmates. The doctor showed me the x-ray of where I had fractured my hand. They gave me a little cast and told me it would have to heal on its own. My grandfather really wasn't mad at me; it's a good thing I could talk to him about anything and I told him what was going on ahead of time.

While I was suspended I got a phone call from the school asking me and my mother to come up to the school for a meeting. They told me that with my history, I couldn't return to the school for the rest of the year. Since I ran out of options for schools I could go to, I failed the seventh grade. There was no way I could make up all those classes in summer school. You want to know what's more embarrassing than getting hit in the face and having your class laugh at you? Failing and the first day back to school having to watch your old classmates go to the next grade. In the end, my classmates were still laughing at me; I didn't exactly see them laughing, but I always felt like they were behind my back. Then the most painful part about failing a grade is when the class you were supposed to be in graduates. All you can think about is that could have been you walking across that stage moving on to high school. I'm slightly glad it happened, though, because my eighth grade teacher was an ex-Black Panther. She was the first person to open my eyes to conspiracy theories, a list of major corporations that were owned by the Illuminati, and all the hidden symbols on the pieces of paper we call money. I didn't know what she was talking about, or if I even believed her. I know now that she wasn't crazy and that everything she tried to show me was real.

After four long years of middle school, I finally graduated. My father started coming around again, and he bought me a pair of Shaq shoes for school. He even took me bowling with him and his new girlfriend. Even though they weren't the most popular gym shoes to wear growing up, those shoes meant more to me than any pair of shoes money could buy. I wore them everywhere until the soles came off the bottoms. Even though all my friends used to always make fun of me, walking behind me saying "Kazaam," I would pay anything to get another pair of those shoes. While in middle school, my mother entered me into a lottery pick to get into a new school designed and funded by one of the Big Three auto companies. The school had just opened up the year before. The school was created by the Ford Motor Company, and its main focus was "Manufacturing Arts and Science" and it was located in a museum. It being a school created by one of the Big Three gave my mother hope that it would create a better opportunity and provide a better future for me. After all, we did live in the Motor City, and all the good jobs you hear about growing up have something to do with the Big Three. She liked the school even more for having a no fighting, zero tolerance policy, because she thought it would keep me out of trouble. I started school, and I quickly learned I had a whole other distraction, girls. I was a virgin who had never done anything more than talk to a girl I met at a bowling party on the phone and to girls that stayed in my neighborhood. I was shy and had no real experience talking to girls, and that was a bad combination. My first day in school, I began to have a crush on a girl in my class. She made me nervous just being around her. I had no idea what to say or do to make her mine. All I knew was when I got home, I couldn't wait to go to school the next day to see her again, in hopes that she would one day notice me. One day, out of the nowhere, she asked me for my phone number. We talked a few times, but she soon broke my heart by getting a boyfriend. It's hard seeing a person you really like with someone else every day. Especially when you know you could or would treat them so much better.

Time went on and I finally started having sex the summer after my tenth grade year, with my good friend and neighbor across the street. Well, really it was just once, considering she told me not to tell anyone and I ended up telling everybody in our neighborhood what happened. She was pissed. I can still hear her voice screaming outside my window. Eventually, she got over it and we became friends again. After having sex for the first time, I returned to school the next semester a sex crazy teenager. That school year, I was completely dedicated to having sex and playing basketball. Between the two, I really didn't have much time on my hands for anything else. I played on the basketball team for three years in high school. I started out my tenth grade season on varsity. I kind of hated it, because since I was tall, they always tried to make me play center. I'm only 6' 4". I am more like a small forward type of guy. So I worked hard to get my game where it needed to be in hopes that one day I could change positions. I came out the next season strong, and I felt invincible on the court. After a few games, my coach changed my position. I was where I wanted to be and had my chance, and just like that, it was over. The game I started in my new position, I stole the ball from the other team. As the person I stole the ball from ran behind me to try to stop me from scoring on a fast break, he tripped me as I was driving towards the rim. Another defender was coming to block me and had already jumped in the air. He ended up coming down on my head and it knocked me out. I had a seizure and a concussion right there on the hardwood floors of the basketball court. I sat out for a few games to recover, but I never really recovered after that day. No matter how bad I wanted to, I never played the same again. I guess I had unknowingly built up a fear of getting hurt again. Somehow, I still ended up with the most improved player award at our basketball banquet at the end of the season. I still stayed on the team, but after the accident, I never really gave it my all anymore. The dream every kid that loves basketball growing up has slowly began to fade away.

After everything that happened, I ended up being in a relationship with one of the cheerleaders. It was the girl I had had a crush on; she had finally noticed me after two years. We stayed together for about nine months, but just like that, I ended it. I realized that I was young, and it was lust not love, and I wanted to experience life. After the breakup, I decided to become the ladies' man at my school. I thought about all the women at my school that I wanted to have sex with. I figured just walking up to them and asking for sex wouldn't work. So I had to figure out a way to make them want to sleep with me without being straight forward. I had to tempt them, so I researched everything about sex online. The school assigned every student a laptop at the beginning of the year that we could take home and use in class. So every night, instead of doing homework, that's what I studied: sex. I came up with a lie about my auntie being a sex therapist. How she taught me everything about a woman's body and different tricks on how to please them in bed. Kind of like a sex education class on how to make women have orgasms quick. My plan worked out nicely, and everything was going as planned. I slept with almost any girl I wanted to that year. The problem was that our school only had a little over 400 students total. People started to notice all the attention I was getting, especially after one of my so-called friends made a flyer about me. The flyer was about two girls I had taken to the movies during a half-off day and talked into getting naked. Everybody thought after the flyer that I had slept with both of the girls. When really we got close, but I couldn't bring myself to take the virginity of a girl I would probably never talk to again or love. The other girl wasn't a virgin, but she started feeling guilty about cheating on her boyfriend, especially since I knew him. It never went further than me seeing them naked. After the flyer incident, my plan started to back fire, and every time a girl skipped or went anywhere with me, people automatically assumed that we had sex. I mean, eight times out of ten they were right, but I didn't want anyone to know. Then one day, some of the senior girls tried to plan a no girls talk to me day. Their plan didn't work, but it certainly made me not really want to go to school anymore.

I was three months away from graduating, and I started skipping so much it was almost impossible for me to graduate. Then I heard my grandfather talking on the phone about how he had promised my dead great-grandfather he would make sure I graduated and how proud of me he was. Hearing that conversation made me feel so bad I felt like I had to graduate. I did everything I could that last month to graduate. I did make-up work, extra credit, and extra homework. After doing everything I could to get my grades up, I finally had the grades to walk across stage. My grandfather had kept his promise. At graduation, they called my name to walk across the stage; the only thing I was thinking while walking across the stage was, don't trip, because everybody is looking at you. When I got to the principle, I turned to look at the crowd. Everyone was clapping. Then I turned and looked where my family was sitting. I knew I had made them proud, and the look on my grandfather's face was priceless. After the ceremony, I walked to the front of the museum to get my report card. I had never seen so many D minuses on one report card in my life. I didn't want to mess up the celebration, so I took the report card and tucked it safely in my pants pocket. I thought high school was the hardest thing I would ever have to do. That college would be fun and a breeze since I didn't have to go so much. That being an adult would be easy and I would be glad to have my freedom and to be on my own. Little did I know that being an adult isn't easy, that life can be hard, and sometimes it can seem as though it's unfair. Through my experience, you just have to take the good with the bad and live life. When life gives you more bad than good, you just have to hope tomorrow is better than today and believe everything happens for a reason and that God can bring you out of any situation if you trust in him. Especially the situations I have been in as an adult, because now that I looked back, I realize only God could have brought me through.

CHAPTER 2

DOING WHAT I FELT I HAD TO

I started my adulthood by going to a community college a few miles away from where I lived. I didn't fill out any applications for any university's or take my SATs or ACTs. I never really even thought about college in high school. So community college or trade schools were really my only two options for a better education. Even though I was grown by law, I guess you couldn't really call me an adult, because I still stayed at home with my mother. The college life lasted only a few weeks. It didn't work out exactly how I planned it. The biggest problem I had started because I couldn't figure out what it was that I wanted to go to college for. That's probably why, in my mind, I started to look at college as a waste of time. I can't tell you how many people I know who graduated from college and still don't make enough to be considered middle class or who are unemployed. Most people grow up wanting to own a business or be a doctor or lawyer, or they want to go into the family business. You know, be what they always wanted to be. Me, all I ever wanted to be was rich, because I thought being rich meant being free. I knew I didn't want to have to go through life struggling, living from check to check, and I guess I just wanted to be loved by everybody. It was that feeling of being unsure that led to the next problem, and that was all the freedom I was given at college. Nobody was going to call my mother if I didn't show up. None of the teachers really cared if I attended their classes. I showed up to my classes for about two weeks, until I made friends. Then I found myself ditching class to stand around the student center laughing and joking around. I ended up failing every class but weight training. I think that teacher got me confused with somebody else, because I barely went to that class either. I was able to drop one of the classes so it wouldn't be as bad. I still felt bad, though, because it was my first semester in college, and I didn't even make it through. It was my first semester, and it would be my last semester in community college. I felt like a failure at first, but I realized that I was happy with my raggedy but running car, the clothes I was wearing, and living in my mother's basement.

Around that time, my best friend, Brittney, introduced me to a girl named Turtle. She was so beautiful inside and out. She was the type of girl you would want to marry, settle down with, and have kids with. I could picture myself with her in that nice, big house with the white picket fence and our kids running around playing in the yard. Even though bad things always seemed to happen in her life, she always found a way to be happy. It was like nothing got to her. I could be myself with her, and loving her made me feel free for the first time in my life. I started to see life differently, I loved everything about her, I felt alive inside. Even the air I was breathing felt different; she made me want to be better. I figured out there are things that are way more important in life than money, but I knew I needed some pocket change to have gas money to go see her, so I decided to get a job. I started working as a security guard, and I took a second job at a department store. It put a little money in my pocket, but I was still always broke, even living at my mother's house. Working two jobs was cool, but it took away from the time I got to spend with Turtle. I quit the department store job after about two months, because I barely got to see her and I missed spending time with her. It's all I ever looked forward to doing. I wanted to marry her, but then the talk about her going to college came up. She wanted to go to a college in Florida; it was her dream and she was tired of Michigan. I didn't have money to move to Florida. I was a security guard making minimum wage. My raggedy car wouldn't have made it to Ohio, which was only like forty-five minutes away. I had lived in Detroit all my life and I didn't know anything else. I wasn't ready to leave my family or friends, but I would have done anything for her.

Instead of trying to tell her I was happy for her, I called my best friend to ask for her advice and to vent. I got pissed and said a lot of things, not so much out of anger, but because I was hurt. I felt like she was leaving me, and I was afraid of being alone again. Then, just like that, my best friend betrayed me by telling Turtle everything the next day. I mean, she did bring us together, so I guess she felt responsible for the outcome of our relationship. She looked at it from the woman's perspective, and I was wrong for what I said, but I would have never thought she would have broken the unspoken code between best friends. When Turtle called me, mad about what she had heard, my ego took over. I told her to make a choice, that if she loved me, she would go to a college closer to home. I forced her to break up with me, and she didn't want to. She wanted to stay together. I see now how selfish I was then, but it is too late now. My ego was the cause of us breaking up, and we never recovered. My love for her stayed, but she was gone forever. I lived for years with regret, wondering every day what would have happened if I had handled things differently. It took me five years to get over her, and she will always have a special place in my heart.

I had never felt so alone in my life. I told myself that I would get my life together while she was gone. That the next time I was in a serious relationship, whether it be with her or someone else, I would be ready. I would love, protect, and be able to provide for her. I would never be in a relationship again without having money. After all, the only way to provide for your family nowadays is by having a lot of money. This so-called civilized world we live in has taken the freedom to do anything ourselves anymore; we depend on money and technology for everything. I didn't know how I was going to do it. I just knew that I had to. I knew with no job skills, a regular nine-to-five job wouldn't cut it. I needed money fast, so I tried just about every hustle I could think of doing. Since Thomas had just come out of jail after doing ten years, it wouldn't be hard. Thomas was the guy my mother met after Keith. He lived a street life and was a hustler. My mother had a thing for guys like that, considering she stayed with my father for so long. Thomas went to jail because he was ordering cars with rich people's credit cards and got caught. He didn't snitch on how he got the information or anybody involved. So they tried to lose him in the prison system. Ten years for stealing a car is a little harsh, don't you think, but still my mother waited for him. If that isn't real love, then I don't know what is. I guess he still had connections on the outside, because when he got out, he hit a couple corners and was right back to the money. He took some of the money he collected and invested it in me. He didn't really have a plan when he got out, so he believed in mine.

I threw a party in hopes of making money, but my cell phone got cut off the day of the party. Nobody showed up: twelve hundred dollars down the drain. I guess party promoting just wasn't in my blood. Then I tried to get back some of the money I lost by trying to sell weed, but my car broke down. All the people I knew that smoked stayed too far away. I really didn't know too many people that smoked weed in the neighborhood we moved in. It took me so long to get it off, I ended up spending the money, slowly but surely. Thomas didn't say anything, but I could tell he was pissed about me not having the re-up money. After all, that something bad still had to happen. I guess the saying is true: "When it rains it pours." The guy we had been paying rent to for a year wasn't paying the property taxes on the house. We got evicted by the city, and all the pressure was on Thomas to make something happen. He used the money he had left, along with one of my mother's paychecks to move into a big house in the suburbs. It was what my mother always wanted: to live in a big house that she owned. My mother had a good job, but with that big mortgage, her paychecks just weren't enough. So Thomas tried to start a lawn care service. It worked out pretty well for a while, giving him a little extra money here and there, but Thomas wasn't used to living check to check. He was used to getting fast money and living comfortably without worries. The lawn service was good, but as with any business, some people didn't pay or didn't pay on time.

Then the worst possible thing happened: my mother lost her job as the supervisor at a health care company. The company had to lay off some employees and the supervisors were the first to go. The pressure was on again, and Thomas started trying to think of ways to get money, but none of them were legal ways. We talked him out of doing something stupid, especially since he thought technology hadn't grown over the ten years he was in prison. So he tried to get a job, but nobody would hire a convicted felon. A few months later, the police raided the house and took him to jail. His friend got caught doing something illegal and snitched on him. Nobody knows whether he did what they say he did or not. All I know is he went back to prison for another ten after being free for almost two years. Even though my mother's heart was broken again, I don't blame him for what he did. You can never say what anyone is capable of doing when it comes to your family's survival. Who knows, I probably would have done the same thing for my family. Thomas was real in my opinion, but I wish he could have found another way. When I get some money, I plan on putting something on his books in prison.

I was broke and alone, my mother was losing her house, and I was jobless. I heard about a trade school near my grandmother's house that was good. I needed something, anything to believe in at the moment. So I moved in with my grandparents the next week. After I passed the enrollment test, I began going to trade school to be a machinist. Motivated by family and love, but still facing the fact the woman I loved was gone, I managed to get really good grades in school. I got halfway through the program, and one day, I started having really bad stomach pains. I had to leave school early. Later that night, my mother came to the house and rushed me to the hospital. When I got to the emergency room, they forced me to drink this liquid that tasted like cold, black coffee with no cream or sugar. When my x-ray came back, they informed me I had to have my appendix removed, and that if I had waited any longer, it would have been too late. While in the hospital, a nurse told me that nobody knows what an appendix does, but when it goes bad, it has to be removed, because it releases poison into the body. I sat in the hospital wondering why it had to happen to me while I was in school. All I could think was, *Why me, Lord; all I was trying to do was something positive with my life.* When I went back up to the school after I got out of the hospital, they told me I would have to wait until the next class started. There I was, held back a class again, not for fighting a bully this time, but for a reason that I couldn't control.

After school one day, my grandmother was late picking me up. I waited out by the curb in front of the school so I could see her car coming. A Rover passed by, and the guy next to me said, "I can't wait until the day I can afford one of those." That being my favorite truck, I agreed. The next day, I figured out he was in the next class I had to join to graduate. He was the only person I knew starting my new class and we quickly became good friends. Soon after, I figured out he was just as smart as me. He was just a different kind of smart. See, PJ was from the streets. He stayed in a much rougher part of the city. We stayed off the same main street, but his hood was a lot worse than mine when it came to violence and drugs. He dropped out of middle school to sell crack when he was twelve. He never spent one day in high school, and when I met him, he had still never seen what the inside of a high school looked like. He went to a GED program when he was fifteen and could read a book, learn, and comprehend anything he wanted to know. See, me, I hated reading, but I could see or hear something and remember it and analyze it, plus I took good notes. We had the same dreams and motivation at the time, and that was making money and getting our lives together. In school, a lot of times I got better grades. He was still in the high 90s on the tests, and he never had the advantages of being in high school. At the trade school we went to, classes started off with about eighty people, but only about twelve out of every class graduated. In every class that graduated, somebody was awarded a Kennedy toolbox as an award for being the top student in three categories: attitude, attendance, and academics. Never in the history of the school has there been a tie. We tied for the award, both receiving a toolbox, even though my grades were slightly higher. I had a bad attitude, but I was going through a lot and nobody knew my pain. It was the first tie in the school's history and the last. They figured out a way to break the tie after that for the top student.

I got out of school and the job placement got me a job making the same amount of money I would've probably been making if I hadn't gone to school. I needed to make more money, and finding an entry level job didn't pay exactly what I wanted to get, so I used the job for experience. I started getting my checks and going to the hood and gambling. I started shooting dice every day, and even though I lost most of the time, I was pulled by the thought that today might be my day to hit big. I had a gambling problem, but I didn't realize it until the day I lost everything. I ended up losing all my money and quitting my job, because I didn't have enough gas to make it back and forth to work. You would have thought that I had learned my lesson, considering my father was killed at an after-hour dice game on Detroit's east side. I even lost a good friend over a dice game because of a disagreement. We got into a fist fight, and later he and his family came back for revenge. They tried to jump me and my brother that night. I see how stupid it was now to fight a friend, especially for something as little as a dollar. Even though the fight wasn't about the dollar at all; it was about pride.

After that I decided that I would only gamble at the casino, but in the casino, you lose your money a whole lot faster. After losing everything again, I finally decided to quit gambling and get myself together, because nothing good ever came from it, at least not for me. I started looking for another job and hanging out with PJ and the people from his hood. I thought I lived in the hood; where I was from was like paradise compared to where they lived. They were a whole different type of people, and I respected them for who they were, and they respected me for who I was. They were like a pack of wild wolves that stuck together no matter what. Even if they fought against each other, they fought until first blood, and then it was over. They went and got a drink and forgot about it. Then the next day, they acted as if it never happened. Money and violence were like meat to them, and they ate it on a regular basis. If somebody had any type of problem with any of them, they definitely finished it without any hesitation. There was always something fun happening in the hood, some party to go to or some women coming over. Anything could happen in the hood, good or bad, at any given time on any given day. I think that's why everybody in the hood either smoked cigarettes, did weed, or drank a lot, because they never knew what was going to happen or if today would be their last. I realized that for some people, being raised in that type of environment was all they knew.

After being in the hood so long, missing shootouts, getting stretched by the police, and being trapped in houses surrounded by dirty cops and not knowing if I was going to make it out, I took a deep breath and remembered what my mother told me about ending up dead or in jail. I decided to get a change of scenery and moved in with my uncle, out of town in Indianapolis, Indiana. Indianapolis was a mix between the city life and the country life. Since I had lived in Detroit my whole life, I only knew the city part of it. The country part was peaceful and sometimes boring to someone who had lived in a city his entire life. It was a lot slower, but maybe that was exactly what I needed: to slow down. It was harder to find a job there. They didn't have a whole lot of jobs for machinists. It wasn't really an industrial city like home, and since I didn't have a car, I had to find somewhere close so I could get a ride from my uncle to and from work. I finally found a job, but since I didn't know how to program the machines, I still ended up making almost minimum wage. After getting the job, a few weeks passed, and I could feel the pressure for me to leave my uncle's house and get my own place. It wasn't from my Uncle Byron, but from his wife, Gina. She had been badmouthing me to family members behind my back, so I left. I met an older woman down there and moved in with her and her four kids. I don't know what qualifies a woman as a cougar, but she was about eight years older than me. It was cool, but she had a dog, and I really didn't like pets, because I am allergic to dog hair. I took a few trips to the hospital while living with her, because my eyes were swollen, I kept throwing up, or I couldn't breathe.

The best part about living with her was she was way more experienced in the bedroom than I was. All this time, I thought I was good in bed, until I met her. She taught me all types of things and different positions. I learned everything I could. The problem started when I started to get curious on whether the techniques she taught me would work on another woman. I started cheating on her, and I thought I would feel bad about it, but my heart was still broken from what happened with Turtle. I realized I didn't care, and I couldn't bring myself to have real emotions for her, no matter how much I tried. I loved her because she was a good person, but my heart wasn't in love with her. It was still cold. That's part of the reason, deep down, I wish we could try again now that I am older and over my past. After cheating a few times, I got my answer: it worked, and I decided that I would stop cheating. She started to ask questions about where I was and who was calling my phone. I didn't want to hurt her feelings, plus I had nowhere else to stay, so I lied. It was too late, though; she looked through my phone and saw a text from a girl saying, "hey babe." After that, we got into a big argument, and she put me out of her house. So I gathered my things, packed my bags, and left. I ended up moving back home to Detroit with my mother, because I knew I couldn't go back to live with my Uncle Byron. I wasn't mad at her decision; I was wrong. Plus I was homesick. I missed my family back in Detroit.

My mother still stayed in her big house, but she hadn't paid the mortgage in months. The first thing I tried to do when I got home was get a job. I applied just about everywhere, but nobody would hire me. Suddenly, I knew how Thomas felt when he was looking for a job. I even went back to the job placement department at my school, but I didn't even get a call back. After searching for a while, I found a job just outside of Dayton, Ohio. I had my interview and they hired me over the phone. They set me up with a plane ticket and paid for my stay at a three star hotel. I was doing well, and I saved up about ten grand in a few months. That was the most money I had ever seen or had in my life. I know it's not a lot, but to somebody that was down bad like I was, I felt rich. I felt like I was on top of the world and living the American Dream. It felt good to finally have money in my pocket. I had a nice car with rims; it had a TV radio in it, and I had sounds in my trunk to go along with it. I was fresh from head to toe, and I had money in my pocket. After getting everything I wanted at the time, I began to realize something. All the material things I bought didn't matter to me as much as I thought they would, and I still felt the same.

I mean, not being broke felt great, but spending money on things I really didn't need didn't make me feel better. I wasn't broke and I had all these new friends that seemed like they came out of nowhere, but a big part of me still felt lonely, and I wasn't happy. I still felt like there was something or someone missing in my life. I felt empty inside. So I started going to neighborhood bars and strip clubs in Dayton, Ohio. I had hit a couple of bars before, but my first night at the strip club, I went by myself. It was sort of a last minute thing and I didn't plan on being in there a long time. When I got there, I ordered a bottle of champagne. I sat about seven hundred dollars in singles on my table to give the dancers the illusion I was going to tip it all to them. As I sat there, I drank the whole bottle of champagne straight out of the bottle, by myself. I tipped a little bit of the money and then stuffed the majority of the money from the table back in my pocket. Everybody thinks you threw all the money, but really, I left with about four hundred dollars of the money from the table stuffed back into my pockets by the end of the night. With the money just sitting on the table like that, just about every exotic dancer in the club approached me that night. I knew why they were there, and just about every last one of them gave me their life story and attempted to sell me a dream. They all offered me their numbers, hoping I would call.

They were all so beautiful, but the one I really wanted made me wait to get her number. She told me if I ever saw her again that it was meant for me to have it. I thought she was just trying to sucker me back up there to tip her again. She was attractive, and if she was setting some type of trap for me, I fell for it. I don't know if it was the fact that she made me wait or if it was because she reminded me of my favorite porn star. I just know she was thick in all the right places with a nice smile. I had to have her, so I came back the next week. She told me it was her third time dancing, and I could tell she was telling me the truth. Even though part of a stripper's job is telling you what you want to hear, the fact that she was kind of clumsy and couldn't really dance didn't lie. I got her number, and two weeks later, I convinced her to stop dancing. We hit it off at first, but when you first meet a person, you can really only go off what they tell you. It takes time to figure out who a person really is, because most people don't show you who they really are in the beginning of a relationship. Who knew the person she portrayed to be was a complete lie? I sold her a dream and she sold a bigger one right back. That person she really was, was exactly who your mother warned you to stay away from. I barely knew her, and I had her staying at my hotel room while I was at work. At my job, I worked seven days a week, twelve hours a day, and when I came home, I was exhausted. I really never spent time with her, even though I always wanted to. Sometimes I got back to the room and went straight to sleep. I woke up one day and went to the bathroom and noticed sex stains on my shirt. I didn't remember having sex with her, so I asked her what happened. She explained to me that she had been having sex with me while I was asleep. I knew I was a hard sleeper, but I couldn't believe I slept through sex. I don't know whether she was trying to trap me or whether I was caught in the lustful fantasy of her, but after a month or two of dating, she was pregnant. After we found out, all I knew was that the more I got to know her, the further she seemed from the person I couldn't wait to get home and see every day.

We started arguing a lot, and it was mostly because she lied about everything, whether it was big or small. I loved her for the fact my son was growing in her stomach, but most of the time, I was miserable when I was around her. I could barely stand to hear the sound of her voice. We got into a big argument one day, and I got tired of her lies. I needed some time to cool off away from her so I could think. So I left for Detroit to surprise my mother for her birthday. I didn't tell her why I left, but she thought I wasn't coming back, at least that was her story, even though I still had a lot of my belongings and clothes there. She called me the day after and told me she had been comforted by her ex-boyfriend. I was so hurt, all I could think about was getting revenge, so I called Turtle. She spent the night with me at a friend's house in the hood. Although revenge felt so good, and for a moment I was happy again, I woke up the next morning with the harsh reality that my girlfriend cheated on me while she was pregnant with my unborn son. But still, I had a smile on my face, because I was with Turtle.

I had a hard decision to make; did I try to get back with the woman I had loved for so long or try to make things work between me and the mother of my child. The only thing that helped me get over Turtle was that she had finally let the ups and downs of life get to her. She was no longer the beautiful, kind woman I used to know, the person I fell in love with. I mean, I know she was still that same person somewhere on the inside, but I had to try to make things work. I decided I would try to be a family for the baby. So I rushed back to Ohio to try to make things right. Things never really got right, though. I always had that thought of her being with another man in the back of my mind haunting me like nightmare. She asked me what I did when I went to Detroit. I lied straight to her face and told her nothing. I guess I wanted to make her feel bad for what she had done, and since she always lied, I didn't feel bad about it.

A few weeks went by and it ended up coming out during an argument anyway. We got into it, and I told her the truth about what had happened when I went home. Just like a man, getting mad and telling on myself. She broke out crying, and the next day she ended up having contractions. She had to be rushed to the hospital. She stayed on bed rest for a while in the hospital. They told us she had complications and that the baby was trying to come early. I couldn't help but think that it was my fault that my son came early. Between me coming clean about getting revenge and us getting into fights, I couldn't but think that's what caused it. One time, I even put my hands on her and hit her back when she hit me in the face with a purse for playing around too much. I still feel bad about that to this day, but I can never take back my actions, no matter how many times I apologize. She stayed in the hospital for about a week, and then it happened. My son was born at twenty-four weeks and diagnosed with sickle cell anemia. He was one pound seven ounces at birth; my hand was bigger than him. His eyes were still fused shut and we couldn't even touch his skin because it bruised easy. He stayed in the hospital for four and a half months, and seeing him hooked up to all those machines, wondering if he was going to make it was one of the scariest and most painful things that could ever happen to a parent. When our miracle was well enough, they finally let him come home on a breathing machine. You would have thought that with everything that happened it would have brought us closer together as parents, but it seemed as though things only got worse for us as a family. When my son came home, I decided that we needed the help and support of family. I was scared, and even though I was good with kids, I wasn't fully ready for the responsibility of raising a child. So I found a job and moved my son and his mother, Eve, back to Detroit.

Eve was an orphan growing up. Her mother got hooked on drugs, so she lived in foster homes most of her life. I realize now that's why she lied so much; she was looking for me to except her, and I don't think I ever did that or made her feel comfortable to be herself around me. Her childhood was filled with so much pain, and I would have been just as afraid to show anyone who I was too. You heard about my childhood, and even still, I'm sometimes afraid to show people who I really am for fear of rejection. She never really had a stable family environment, except for her last foster home, but even they had their problems. I figured, she was the mother of my child, she was family, and my family would welcome her with open arms. I guess it was kind of selfish of me to ask her leave the only home and family she had ever known.

We stayed with my mother for a while, just until I got on my feet. I was hoping while we were there she would find comfort in making my family her own. It started off good, until I quit my job after a few weeks. I made good money, but my boss hated me, and I didn't know why. It made me feel uncomfortable, and instead of doing what I had to for my family, I quit. Since I didn't have a job, I never got on my feet for my family. I got comfortable again being in my mother's house. We ended up being in that situation for about six months, maybe even longer. The longer we stayed with my family, the further we moved apart. When I finally found a job, I moved out into a party house with my friends from my old neighborhood, because the rent was cheap. As for her and the baby, they ended up taking over the lease on a friend of mine's apartment. The more we moved apart, I realized the only reason I wanted to be with her so bad was because I didn't want anyone else to have her. I was confused, but deep down inside I knew she wasn't the one for me. We started seeing other people, and she found a female friend to go out with. She always wanted to go out and get away from the apartment, so I spent a lot of time there at first. I guess with us not being together and her being in a new place, she was lonely. I've moved to enough places in my life to know the feeling.

Eventually, living at the party house came to an end. Somebody, or one of my roommates, stole all my things while I was at work. I had to start over again with nothing, and I didn't feel comfortable staying in that house. So I slowly moved in with my son's mother, and since I was always there anyway, I figured it wouldn't be a problem. Even though we still had sex from time to time, I still slept in the living room on the couch. My son always slept in the living room with me, on my chest, and when I wasn't there, he still slept on the couch from time to time. Then she started going out of town and leaving me and our son together. She would leave for months at a time. At first she was leaving to go on a job she had back in Ohio. Then she started leaving to go with her sister. See, her sister was a model, and she messed with a lot of stars, famous people, and people with money. She was a full-blown groupie, but she called herself a vixen. So you never knew what state she was in, which star she was with, or which one of his boys she was talking to at the time. Me being a single father, and that being my first child, I didn't always know what to do, but I did the best I could. I think the longest she left with her sister was about six months, but she always called to speak to our two-year-old son.

After all the times she went out of town with her sister, she stopped going to see her. She came back for a while, then started leaving to go see a guy she had met at the bus station one of the times she went to visit her foster family in Ohio. He lived all the way in Atlanta, but he was a rapper, so he was in Detroit sometimes. The point is, out of the two years she stayed in Detroit, she was maybe there thirteen of the months. I realized that she was young and hadn't experienced life yet and that our family was broken and would never be fixed. Sometimes I used to think that one day she was going to leave and never come back, and just leave me and my son together. When she came back for the last time, we started arguing again. It was mainly because she was gone so long and had lied about how long she was leaving for. She said her reason for being gone for three months the most recent time was because her birth mother was dying. I mean, who lies about something like that? Another reason we were arguing was because I couldn't get my friend to re-do the renters insurance on the apartment where we stayed, since the apartment was still in their name. The rental office was threatening to evict us if we didn't get it. It was part of their policy to make sure all the tenants had it. I was angry and didn't really communicate what was going on to her. So a few days after she came into town, I got a private phone call, and it was her. She told me she and my son were on the freeway and that she had changed her number. Just like that, my son was gone. I went back to the apartment and she had taken what she could and left.

I was crushed that she had taken my life away from me. All I kept thinking was how I wished I had signed his birth certificate. I signed the paper, but the woman that notarized it was on vacation from the hospital. I never pushed to have my name on it, because I didn't want to pay child support for my son, who I took care of anyway. When my family found out he was gone, they told me to call the police, but I never did. My mother, on the other hand, told me to let them go. I think she knew I was struggling as a father. I told myself my son and his mom would be back in a weeks. After a few weeks, she finally called, and I begged her to let me talk to my son. Then I asked what state they were living in. At first she lied and told me they moved back to Ohio, when she really moved to Atlanta to stay with the guy she had met at the bus station. I missed my son's third birthday; I tried to act like I was fine, but I ended up breaking down crying while I was driving. I had to pull over to the side of the road until I got myself together. I never thought that I would ever miss one of his birthdays, or any other part of his life for that matter. I was alone again, but this time I was filled with a lot of different emotions; the biggest one was anger. I didn't know what God's plan was for me, and even though I had talked about writing a book, I didn't really start writing until my son was taken away. I guess that was the push I needed to start doing what I felt I had to do.

After she moved, though, everything bad that could happen did. I lost my job at the research laboratory and had to get on unemployment. My company was doing badly, especially since the main companies they worked and tested parts for were the Big Three. All the car companies were in a crisis, and the economy slipped into a recession. Nobody was buying cars. I couldn't stand to be in the apartment, because I kept waking up in the morning looking for my son. So I rented out a room on the east side, but most of the time, I stayed with my mother at her new apartment. I had never stayed on the east side before, but I had heard stories about it. It wasn't my hood or anywhere I felt was familiar, so I really didn't feel comfortable being there. After a few months, my mother wanted to move out of the apartment she was in, but ended up getting evicted first. She got evicted because of problems with the paperwork in the rental office. While we were searching through our things, seeing what we could take with us in the car and trying to figure out whether the people who set our stuff out had taken anything, my mother realized they had stolen a lot of our things, including the four hundred dollars she had put away in her dresser. I don't know which one of us did it, but we were passing a cigarette around, and either somebody dropped it or set it down in the storage bin and wasn't paying attention. All I know is, all of our things caught on fire right in front of our eyes as we were looking through our things and my mother broke out crying. The flames quickly spread throughout all of our possessions and memories. I hadn't seen her cry like that since the day I got put out of Detroit Public Schools.

I did the worst thing I could possibly do in that situation: I started gambling again, hoping for a miracle. I lost my rent money at the casino and had to move in with my brother. My ex-landlord, who was a friend from the neighborhood I grew up in, was threatening me about rent money, but I didn't care. I felt like I had nothing to lose anyway. I was broke for two weeks until my next unemployment check came. I tried to stack and put some money away to move out of my brother's townhouse, because he had a family of his own. It seemed like the more I tried to save, the more something always came up where I had to spend money. After moving into my brother's townhouse, I went to go pick up Turtle and take her to work one day. We were just friends now, and she needed a favor. On my way home from dropping her off, my car broke down on the freeway. My engine went out and I had no real money to get it fixed. On top of that, I had to go get my son from out of town, which wasn't a bad thing; I just wasn't prepared. I was doing badly myself and was in no condition to take care of him. But my son's mother ended up being pregnant again and had to be on bed rest at the hospital, so I really didn't have a choice. So I did what any real man would do. I forgot about my problems and focused on him. I left for Atlanta the next day and it was a two-day ride. I almost made it to my destination, but then I ended up getting into an accident. I left the scene in an ambulance to the hospital. Because of the accident, I paid somebody my son's mom knew two hundred dollars to pick me up from Tennessee and take me to Atlanta. I have two discs in my back that will never be the same again.

I picked my son up in August, and I had to leave my brother's house in November. His daughter needed a new heart, and there were just too many people in one townhouse. I decided I wasn't going to let my son live in the hood, so I moved into a hotel room right outside of the city. We stayed there for a month and a half, until his grandfather on his mother's side came to get him and take him back to Atlanta right after Christmas. Her biological father had come back into her life after years of not talking and was willing to do anything to make things right. So picking my son up was just one of the things he felt like he could do to gain the trust and love of his daughter back. I didn't want my son to go, but with my back injury and not having a stable place to stay, it was the best thing for him. It's hard running after a four-year-old when you walk with a cane. I took him shopping before he left and my family came together too so he wouldn't need anything when he got there. After he left, all I did was go to physical therapy and stay in the house. I had nothing but time on my hands.

After the fire, my mother ended up meeting someone and getting married for the first time in her life, to a guy who is good for her, who loves her, and who does things the legal way. My son's mom and I have a good relationship now. We argue at times, but I guess that's what parents do. We keep it civil for my son most of the time, but since he is down there, she always treats everything like she's in control and there is nothing I can do about it. She married the guy from the bus station. They have a family together and she turned out to be a great mother to my son. My son is in school now and doing well, thanks to her. Even though we argue, I wouldn't trade her as my son's mother if I could. She says he talks about me all the time and she sometimes encourages me to be a better father, even though I sometimes don't feel like much of a father at all, because we live about 1,000 miles apart from each other. I feel like I am missing a big part of his life. I know in my heart I want to be a better father, but it seems as though me and my son's mom traded places and I'm the one who's never there. I find it difficult, because sometimes I hear my son call another man dad in the background when we're on the phone. We don't talk that much on the phone, even though I think about him all the time. I hope one day to move closer so I can help raise him to be a man.

> Son, if you grow up to read this book one day and I'm not around, just know that I miss you, and all the best times in my life were when we were together. I still watch your favorite TV show without you sometimes and pretend like your right here next to me. I love you with all my heart and I can't wait till the day we are together as a family, father and son.

My niece got a new heart and is now recovering and doing well.

My best friend and I are still close, and we hang out from time to time. Turtle ended up having a baby, and her daughter is by far the best thing that has ever happened to her. She is back to being that beautiful person I loved and something even more. I've wondered why things turned out this way. I try to find a purpose or some type of meaning to life, wondering what I have been doing wrong and sometimes what I have been doing right. Wondering which direction in life to turn to, and if I can't figure it out, to trust that God will guide me the right way. I know that my life hasn't been perfect, and it never will be as long as I keep thinking the way I do. I know that sometimes I do wrong, but after everything I have done and all that I have been through, I know God is with me always, and there's nothing I can't do with him by my side. Now that he has shown me the way and opened my eyes up to the truth, I know my purpose in life, and I want to share this message God has given to me with you.

CHAPTER 3

MY SECRET AND THE MEANING

One summer night, I grabbed my car keys, got in the car, and started driving. I had no destination in mind, nowhere to be at the time, and no specific route to take. I was cruising around the city, staring out the window, daydreaming about life. It's amazing the things that you see or find when you look hard enough. When you look out into the streets of Detroit, you see a little bit of everything. I don't mean to make the place I've lived in basically my whole life sound bad, but it is what it is. I would say it's not the most peaceful place to grow up in, but it's definitely not how everyone else views us. I saw a news report on TV not that long ago that compared Detroit to Iraq, a country we were at war with at the time. Even though the grass didn't get cut by the city, there were a few abandoned houses in some neighborhoods, and, the more I think about it, in some places it did kind of look like a war zone, it was nowhere near it. Come on now. I mean, we weren't that bad. They make it seem like we can't even go outside without carrying a weapon. We really don't have gangs here and really the only people that have problems here are the people that want them, or people with money. I say people with money only because Detroit was a city of greed. Everybody in the city was trying to live the American Dream and get paid, but to compare us to a country at war is just a little bit harsh, don't you think?

I wrote the above part of my book when I first started writing this book almost three years ago, and I'm sorry to say I may have spoken to soon. The police have even started handing out fliers that say, "Enter Detroit at your own risk." Every day it seems like everything is getting worse and nothing is getting better. Poverty is growing, and it seems as though the people in this city are becoming more cruel and heartless. I saw a show on TV talking about how long it would take for people to turn violent if the world ran out of things like food and clean water. They stated that it would take the world four days to turn violent. Those statistics made me wonder how long it took for these people running the streets now, those who are now living in poverty and struggling to survive, to turn violent. The cost of living is constantly going up, and things like food, water, and gas are becoming things even middle class people can't afford. People are not only killing over greed now, they are killing for their own survival and acting like animals who were raised by a cruel owner. People are desperate and struggling to feed their families now. They are preying on the weak, and our elderly are being robbed and killed for money. Children are turning up dead everywhere and some are still missing. Some children fall victim to senseless acts of violence that they had nothing to do with, and some are slain by the hands of their own parents. It is because either their parents are getting stressed about life and deciding to hurt or end their children's precious lives, or they fear that they may not be able to provide an adequate living environment for them. Children are going hungry and parents are desperately trying to find ways to feed themselves and their families. I have even heard stories of people eating rats for survival. People are committing suicide all across the world, unable to cope with their living conditions and the cards that life has dealt.

I have never in my life heard about so many robberies where people lost their lives over a few dollars. A friend I grew up with was even gunned down in front of a liquor store for trying to steal some glasses. Sometimes I really can't believe half the stories I hear until I actually see them for myself on the news or right before my very eyes. Bodies are turning up in cars and abandoned houses, strangled to death or set afire and burned beyond recognition. People are shooting and trying to rape defenseless women while they're walking their babies in a stroller around the park. There are so many women selling their bodies for pocket change and putting their lives at risk to survive. Dirty cops are storming communities and taking what they can in fear that tomorrow they may be laid off. Some of the law enforcement agencies are even hurting peaceful protestors for standing up for what they believe is right. People can't leave their homes without someone watching their every move and then trying to break in while they're away. When people move out of their homes, people still break in; they strip the houses for scraps to sell for money, and now there are probably more abandoned houses in the city then anything. A lot of people have been forced out of their homes by banks or because they couldn't afford to pay rent to the landlord. Those people who couldn't find a suitable place to live after being forced out of their homes are now living in abandoned houses, tents, cars, homeless shelters, storm drains, hotels, or wherever else they can find shelter all over the country. Parents are offering their kids up for sexual favors in return for merchandise or money.

About a week ago, one of my good friends even had a crazy man with a knife kick in her door. She was seven months pregnant and he kicked down the door, entered her apartment, pushed her down, and tried to stab her and her unborn baby to death. At the time, she had a group of kids over to play with her five-year-old son. After seeing his mother get pushed down, her son and the other kids started hitting the man. Her son screamed out, "Get off my mommy." The man then turned his attention to the kids and went after them with the knife. When the man went after her son and the other kids, she quickly got up and ran to the closet. She grabbed the gun she had for protection out of the shoe box in the closet and shot the man. None of the kids were hurt. She suffered back pains and a deep cut in her hand from when she fought the man off. We are truly living in a world filled with chaos, and growing up, I would have never guessed that the world we live in would come to this, but it has, and without change, it is only going to get worse. You can't just look at Detroit and say we are the problem, or any other place for that matter, because this is now happening all around the world.

Driving around that night made me remember all the things that I have been through, the things I have seen, places I have been to, and the people I have met along the way of this journey we call life. It also made me think about my secret and wonder if any of it was real, but I will get to that later. All of it made me feel like life was a big puzzle and I would never figure it out. After looking at all that and recent events that had happened, I started to question my faith in God. I mean, I think there is a time in everybody's life that they question the Big Man Upstairs. The main reason I got angry and questioned God was because of the events around the time when I graduated from school. When I couldn't find a job.

I used to go to trade school eight hours a day, five days a week, with no pay. I had no car, so my loving grandmother took me everywhere I needed to go. That is until my mother realized Thomas wasn't getting out of jail and let me use his car. I will never forget and I will always be thankful to my grandmother, because she took me willingly, just because she wanted to see her grandson become successful. Every day when I got home from school I would wash up, change clothes, and then go in the living room to watch a little TV, then I would go around the corner to the park. My grandparents didn't know it, but I went to the park to walk and pray every day after school. It was the only time my mind was clear enough to really pray and talk to God. Sometimes I would walk around the park praying for hours. I guess I was praying for the same thing I figured everybody else probably prays about nowadays. I prayed about love, help finding a good job when I graduated, my family and friends, happiness, guidance, and after I graduated, the victims of Hurricane Katrina.

I graduated in July of 2005, but I was still living with my grandparents when Hurricane Katrina hit. I mean, disasters happened all the time, and it's sad when anybody gets hurt or dies in any situation, especially if it's a loved one. But the thing that really made me sad about Katrina was the amount of time it took to help those people. It made me wish that I could have helped in some type of way, but I was broke, so all I could do was pray. Some of the people who lost their homes in the hurricane moved to Detroit. A few of the victims moved into my neighborhood. It was the first time I had seen firsthand how something like that affected a person. I tried to compare their lives to mine, telling myself things could be worse. Not to seem ungrateful after school, but it wasn't exactly how I planned my life to change for the better when I got out. I was broke, I couldn't find a good job, and I was still loveless. When I finally did find a job, I made my situation worse by being greedy and gambling. So after I moved out of town and that didn't work out, I was kind of depressed. When I got back home from Indianapolis, I searched everywhere and still couldn't find a job. It made me feel like I wasted almost a year of my life going to school. I thought about selling drugs, but I couldn't bring myself to sell drugs for real. I felt guilty just selling weed, so I knew I could never bring myself to sell crack or any other drug on the street.

When I wasn't able to find a job and everything was going wrong, all these mixed emotions came out. I directed all my sadness, anger, pain, and every other emotion I had towards God. Anybody that knew me could tell that something was seriously wrong through my actions, but my mother noticed by the look on my face. So she asked and I replied, "If God created this world, why did he make it so messed up?" I mean, I knew he existed, but I couldn't figure out why he wouldn't help me when I needed him to. He could fix my problems and everybody else's in a matter of seconds, but yet he stood by and watched me suffer. I felt like God had it out for me and that he had decided to kick me while I was down. If this was some type of test of faith, I would fail, because I didn't have the strength to believe in anything at the time. I felt like God had completely forgotten about me. I mean, I was only a guy who walked and talked with him every day.

My mother's reply to everything was simple: she told me to get dressed for church. Even though God and I weren't exactly agreeing on my life at the time, I did it anyway. She told me we would talk about it after church. I sat through service with the hope that when I got out of church my mother would have come up with a solution to my problem. My answer came earlier than expected; it seemed as though every word that came out of the preacher's mouth and every harmonic note that was sung out by the choir was meant for me to hear. I've been talking and asking God for signs and answers all my life. God has a funny way of teaching me lessons and sending me answers through other people, and not just preachers, either; it could be anybody. I realized now that God had been with me my whole life, teaching me and guiding me. The main message in church that Sunday was that no matter what you're going through in your life, God has a plan and is always on time. So we didn't need to talk about anything on the ride home, because I had all my answers. Even though my life seemed like it was spiraling downhill, I felt blessed, and although I still didn't see it, I realized God had plans for me too. I see that now more than ever. So I stopped blaming God and I learned to have patience and to trust in him. When I got home, I started to think about the whole reason I even believed in God and why I had stayed away from church so long. I have always been very spiritual; even when I was a child, my mother stayed in the church. In anything I do in life I always follow my heart. I just never know where it is going to lead me, but it has never led me down the wrong path.

When I was six I had a picture my mother bought for me and my brothers in my room. I think she bought it from the dollar store. She probably doesn't even remember, but it was a picture of God in the clouds looking down on us. I used to look at that picture every day before my mother put the blood of Jesus over me and my brothers. Then she would walk me to school. The blood of Jesus was a scripture in Ephesians about putting on the whole armor of God. She read it to us every day to keep us safe, and instead of just saying amen after the prayer, we said, "Blood of Jesus." Despite being so religious at a young age, I had my doubts about whether God even existed. I mean, I had never seen him before, so I asked God for a sign. You know how they say ask and you shall receive? Well, two weeks later, a lady from church came home from her trip to the motherland, Africa. She was taking pictures out of the plane when she was over the ocean. When she got the pictures developed, she noticed one of the pictures looked like a man in the clouds dressed in a robe with open arms. She only had one copy of the picture made at the time, but after seeing and showing it to the rest of the members in the church, the people at church begged the lady for copies. The next week when my mother got her copy, I finally got a good look at the picture, and it was almost exactly like the picture from my room. I never questioned if God was real, or not anymore, because I asked for a sign and I got it. I only asked if he would help me or not at moments in my life when I felt like I really needed him.

After that, I started having dreams. I think I had my first one when I was seven. I kept my dreams a secret for a while, but after I kept having them, I needed answers. The only person on earth I told about them was my mother. I guess I was looking to understand the dreams, and I felt like she was the only person on earth who could help me figure them out without judging me. She couldn't help, though, and time was the only thing that would help me to figure out what my dreams really meant. I remember waking up in the middle of the night crying, afraid to go back to sleep, and my heart would always be beating really fast. They started off as just dreams, but as I got older, they seemed more like nightmares. In my dreams I saw death, pain, war, sometimes happiness, fear, what looked like heaven in the sky, and this symbol of a triangle, which was marked on everything. I couldn't understand why I had the dreams or what they meant. I realized that because of my dreams, I was afraid to go to church. The longer I stayed away from church, stopped reading the Bible, and talking to God, the more I put God in the back of my mind, and the longer the dreams stayed away. Now that I look back, I realize that I was running from my destiny, because when I got older, I started seeing things on the news and different world events that felt more like memories to me, like I had seen them before. My dreams had started to become a reality and sometimes it felt almost like I was going crazy. Then again, every man of God, including Christ at one point of time, had to be thought of as crazy by the people living in the world. My dreams made me start paying attention more to the things that were happening around the world. I didn't start putting everything together, understanding the purpose of my dreams, or God's plan for me until one night when me, PJ, and the rest of the hood went out to a party.

After the party, we went back to a house in the hood, and everybody was talking, laughing, and joking around. Then everything suddenly got serious after PJ asked two of the simplest but hardest questions to answer. He asked what the meaning of life is, and what it is that God wants us to do. We sat there for a moment in deep thought. We figured the only way to answer that question was to go back to the beginning and think about what God really wanted from us then. In mostly all things, you have to understand the beginning to know the present and plan for the future. So we went all the way to the story of Adam and Eve to try to find answers; after all, that was said to be the beginning of life itself. Most people know the story of Adam and Eve, and if you don't know, it is said that they were the first two people created.

Genesis 2:7

⁷ And the Lord God formed man of dust of the ground, and breathed into his nostrils the breath of life; and man became a living soul.

Genesis 2:15–18

¹⁵ And the Lord God took the man, and put him into the Garden of Eden to dress it and to keep it.

¹⁶ And the Lord God commanded the man, saying, Of every tree of the garden thou mayest freely eat:

¹⁷ But of the tree of the knowledge of good and evil, thou shalt not eat of it: for in the day that thou eatest thereof thou shalt surely die.

¹⁸ And the Lord God said, It is not good that the man should be alone; I will make him and help meet for him.

Genesis 2:21–25

²¹ And the Lord God caused a deep sleep to fall upon Adam, and he slept: and he took one of his ribs, and closed up the flesh instead thereof;

²² And the rib, which the Lord God had taken from man, made he a woman, and brought her unto the man.

²³ And Adam said, This is now bone of my bones, and flesh of my flesh: she shall be called Woman, because she was taken out of Man.

²⁴ Therefore shall a man leave his father and his mother, and shall cleave unto his wife: and they shall be one flesh.

²⁵ And they were both naked, the man and his wife, and were not ashamed.

Genesis 3:1–7

¹ Now the serpent was more subtle than any beast of the field which the Lord God had made. And he said unto the woman, Yea, hath God said, Ye shall not eat of every tree of the garden?

² And the woman said unto the serpent, We may eat of the fruit of the trees of the garden:

³ But of the fruit of the tree which is in the midst of the garden, God hath said, Ye shall not eat of it, neither shall ye touch it, lest ye die.

> *⁴ And the serpent said unto the woman, Ye shall not surely die:*
>
> *⁵ For God doth know that in the day ye eat thereof, then your eyes shall be opened, and ye shall be as gods, knowing good and evil.*
>
> *⁶ And when the woman saw that the tree was good for food, and that it was pleasant to the eyes, and a tree to be desired to make one wise, she took of the fruit thereof, and did eat, and gave also unto her husband with her; and he did eat.*
>
> *⁷ And the eyes of them both were opened, and they knew that they were naked; and they sewed fig leaves together, and made themselves aprons.*

After explaining the story, we stopped to think for a minute. All types of thoughts were running through my mind, but the first thought that popped into my head was the fact that I couldn't believe how religious everybody was; you know, them being wolves and all. The second thing I thought about was whether I knew my purpose in life and if God was directing my life somewhere. I thought about that day in church when I was mad at the world, and I began to ask myself if the answer to PJ's question was part of God's plan for me. Then I thought about the story and we started throwing our ideas out about what the story meant to us. We figured the most important thing about the story was that before eating the forbidden fruit, Adam and Eve were completely free. They didn't stress about anything or have any fear. They were free in their minds, bodies, and spirits. They didn't see life the way we see it in today's times. They just enjoyed the things that God put in place for them. They trusted God to provide them with everything needed to survive. They were made for each other; God created woman out of man, and they loved each other with unconditional love, just as God loved them, and they were happy with just the company of each other. They walked around naked and free without a worry in the world. They followed their hearts in everything they did and not their minds so much, because they had no knowledge of what was good and what was evil. Their whole way of thinking was different; it wasn't about right or wrong, just love, faith, and trust in the creator of life. Then we thought about the fact that if God doesn't make mistakes and if he wanted Adam and Eve to live that way before partaking in the fruit, then that must have been how he originally wanted mankind to live here on earth.

I'm not saying get naked and run out into the streets, but if you decided today to live your life free, to love, to trust, and to have complete faith in God, to forget everything you've ever known, honestly, which of the Ten Commandments could you break? The Ten Commandments were the rules God gave to Moses for us to follow.

> ***Exodus 20:3–17***
> *³ Thou shalt have no other Gods before me.*
> *⁴ Thou shalt not make unto thee any graven images, or any likeness of any thing this is in heaven above, or that is in the earth beneath, or that is in the water under the earth:*
> *⁵ Thou shalt not bow down thyself to them, nor serve them: for I the Lord thy God am a jealous God, visiting the iniquity of the fathers upon the children unto the third and fourth generation of them that hate me;*
> *⁶ And showing mercy unto the thousands of them that love me and keep my commandments.*
> *⁷ Thou shalt not take the name of the Lord thy God in vain; for the Lord will not hold him guiltless that taketh his name in vain.*
> *⁸ Remember the Sabbath day, to keep it holy.*
> *⁹ Six days shalt thou labour, and do all thy work:*
> *¹⁰ But the seventh day is the Sabbath of the Lord thy God: in it thou shalt not do any work, thou, nor thy son, nor thy daughter, thy manservant, nor thy maidservant, nor thy cattle, nor thy stranger that is within thy gates:*
> *¹¹ For in six days the Lord made heaven and earth, the sea,*

and all that in them is, and rested the seventh day: wherefore the Lord blessed the Sabbath day, and hallowed it.

[12] Honour thy father and thy mother: that thy days may be long upon the land which the Lord thy God giveth thee.

[13] Thou shalt not kill.

[14] Thou shalt not commit adultery.

[15] Thou shalt not steal.

[16] Thou shalt not bear false witness against thy neighbor.

[17] Thou shalt not covet thy neighbor's house, thou shalt not covet thy neighbour's wife, nor his manservant, nor his maidservant, nor his ox, nor his ass, nor any thing that is thy neighbour's.

What if you decided to live free, I mean really free, what sins could you commit? If raised to be free, what sins could your children commit? Take a long, hard look at your own life. Now think about someone from an American Indian tribe, African tribe, or any group of people who didn't or don't live with the pleasures of technology or modern advancements. Think about those different groups of people all across the world that live off of the land. Now that you have the picture in your mind, do you honestly think their lives were or are any less happy than yours? They were and are completely happy and their lives were and are so much simpler. If anything, I think they were and are happier. The only reason that we feel like we need the things we have in our lives right now is because it's really the only thing we've ever known. It has been programmed into our minds that in order to be happy we need certain things. I believe that if we reevaluate the basic things that we really need, or the things that we really want, we would see that we don't really need much to be happy. After being borderline homeless before, and by definition I was homeless when I was struggling and living in a hotel room with my son, I realized why Christ loved and favored the poor. When you become homeless or poor, your whole mindset changes. Even though the poor may not realize it, they are closer to living the way God has always wanted mankind to live, a life completely dependent on him. Christ even instructed a rich man to sell everything he had and to give away all of his money to the poor and become poor:

Luke 18:22–25
²² Now when Jesus heard these things, he said unto him, Yet lackest thou one thing: sell all that thou hast, and distribute unto the poor, and thou shalt have treasure in heaven: and come, follow me.
²³ And when he heard this, he was very sorrowful: for he was very rich.
²⁴ And when Jesus saw that he was very sorrowful, he said, How hardly shall they that have riches enter into the kingdom of God!
²⁵ For it is easier for a camel to go through a needle's eye, than for a rich man to enter into the kingdom of God.

When people become or are poor or homeless, they learn one major thing about life and that's that a lot of the things they thought they needed and thought they couldn't live without weren't really important, and that they never really needed those things at all. They fall out of love with the world and more in love with the simple things in life. It is because of this that people sometimes become completely free in their minds, just like I did. It wasn't until I realized the thing keeping me from peace was me, my pride and the things a civilized world teaches you to love. Finding that peace is how most people make it through the harsh reality of being poor or homeless in a civilized world. If they can't find a way to cope with the reality of being homeless or find the peace of knowing they really don't need much to be happy, sorry to say, most people end up on drugs, committing suicide, or mentally insane. If you are thinking of doing something stupid because you don't have all the things a civilized world says you need, maybe you will find comfort in knowing Christ was homeless.

Matthew 8:20
²⁰ *And Jesus saith unto him, The foxes have holes, and the birds of the air have nests; but the Son of man hath not where to lay his head.*

In today's world, the worst part about being homeless is finding something to eat, but you learn how to survive after a while. The embarrassment of when you see someone you know or have to tell people you're homeless, because you know in their minds they are somehow judging you, is also hard. The fact that you sometimes have to ask other people for money and help is hard too. Most of the things I named have to do with pride, but even that fades away. The only reason we even have to ask is because we have forgotten how to do things on our own. This civilized world has made mankind weak and helpless to the things that are to come, but I will tell you about that later.

When you're homeless, sometimes you have to worry about getting out of the cold and finding ways to keep warm in the winter. While you are homeless or when you have it all and are reduced to next to nothing, you start thinking about how foolish you were in the past for wasting money on things you didn't need. Every day you think about all the money you wasted over the years, but when you find peace, you start thinking, "Did I ever really need money at all?" I mean, you're still alive and you're surviving without all the technology and advancements of today. Think about if you lived a normal life in today's world. You know, had a job, money, a house, a car, and a loving family, and everything was going great. But then you lost everything, all your material possessions, and you couldn't pay your mortgage, and you had to end up moving with nothing. You were now poor, homeless, and left with some no-name brand cloths. You had to live in an abandoned house or cabin without electricity out in the country. The house had a fireplace to burn wood to keep you warm. It had land so you could raise animals to eat and feed your family, somewhere to fish, or land to grow a garden for vegetables and fruit to eat. You learned how to make candles, you had oils, or you had some type of lantern so you could see in the dark. You lived near a lake or had a well to get water from to take baths and drink. You didn't have to worry about the stress of paying any bills. You just had you and your family, and you had no cell phones, no computers, or any other form of technology. Would you be able to live that life and be happy? The answer for most people in today's world is absolutely not, they wouldn't be able to live that life. Most people wouldn't last five minutes, judging by how they react to something as little as their cell phones going dead. Well, what if I told you that it was the life God originally wanted us to live; would you be able to do it then?

My life has had its ups and downs, but through it all, it has made me stronger. After leaving the hotel room with my son, I quickly learned that there were so many abandoned houses around that most homeless people just pick a house and squat in it until the bank comes and forces them out. Every time they get put out of one place, they move on to the next one. Then they turn everything on illegally and stay there until they are forced to leave again. I'm squatting in a house now that hasn't had the mortgage paid on it in almost two years, and I am hoping the bank doesn't come for this house anytime soon. I don't have anything now but a few changes of clothes, a warm place to stay, and everything I need to write this book. You see, I really don't have much, because I have found peace, and I am perfectly happy, because I trust God in the path he is leading me on.

The truth about people these days is that most of them are stressed and trapped in their own minds and searching for ways to gain freedom for themselves. From the time you're a child, the only thing you're taught to do is do well in school so that you can get a good job and make money. You're taught that money is your key to happiness and you can't live and be happy without it. That's why money is the root of all evil: it's because in a civilized world money can buy you just about anything. It can make you who you want to be among other people, which is why some people become in love with money.

> **Matthew 6:24–25**
> ²⁴ *No man can serve two masters: for either he will hate the one, and love the other; or else he will hold to the one, and despise the other. Ye cannot serve God and mammon (money).*
> ²⁵ *Therefore I say unto you, Take no thought for your life, what ye shall eat, or what ye shall drink; nor yet for your body, what ye shall put on. Is not the life more than meat, and the body than raiment?*

Now think about what money does to people nowadays. Think about your favorite celebrity, whether it's an actor or musician. Think about politicians, judges, cops, or people in positions of power. Think about people with nice houses, cars, jewelry, or whatever else gives someone the feeling that they have no worries. Now think about if it was you. People start to treat you differently. People love you, worship you, praise you, look up to you; you feel powerful, and it is that feeling that becomes an addiction. When you start to feel superior because of all the wealth, possessions, or that position of power, you become arrogant and foolish. That feeling or thought of superiority is called the Luciferian philosophy. That mankind can become gods through enlightenment, knowledge, power, wealth, and control. That people with a lower social status should look up to and praise those with a higher status for their accomplishments. Money can buy you a lot of things, but what money can't buy you are all the things that can make you truly happy, like God, love, peace, and family. A lot of people believe that you can somehow buy your happiness or find happiness more easily with money. What they don't realize is money is only a temporary happiness and true happiness comes from within. Most people realize after accomplishing their goals and getting the money that they're missing something in their lives, just like I did.

This is why I think that some rich people are miserable, because after they've done everything they wanted with their money, what's next? If they are rich and do find love, then they will always question, why is this person there? Is it because of the person's love for money, possessions, and the growth of social status, or is it the love that two people share through God that is unbreakable? People don't realize that being happy and free is a state of mind and that they can have it without being rich. The only everlasting happiness is through God and that is love. People don't realize that the growth of technology and all the advancements of today have one main purpose and that is making people weak, unable to take care of themselves, and more controlled. It is a concentrated evil, pushing mankind farther away from God and how he wanted us to live. Not because mankind has furthered itself, but because it is completely controlled. Those in power have the goal to make you dependent on man instead of God for everything. For example, if they decided to shut all the power off in the world right now, what do you think the world would be like? I'm sure many would survive, but the truth is that the majority of mankind would perish and destroy each other. Civilization has enslaved our minds and we will always be slaves to it as long as we let money and those who control it run our lives. Most people go through life doing anything to get wealthy. No matter if it's selling drugs, killing, robbing, stealing, overpricing everything, scamming, getting rich off others, taking from the poor, or whatever else it takes to make a profit. Some people even sell their souls for wealth. A dollar is just a piece of paper with ink on it that's worth nothing when you think about it. People talk about being intelligent, but in my opinion, the smarter we become over time, the harder life is getting. The only thing that we lose every day and don't even realize we're losing is the ability to live our lives free. We have become in love with the world and have unknowingly moved farther away from what God wanted for us.

1 John 2:15
15 Love not the world, neither the things that are in the world. If any man love the world, the love of the Father is not in him.

Every day we gain more knowledge and come up with new plans and ideas. In return for these new inventions, better technologies, laws, and more efficient ways to be safe, we basically lose our freedom. When I say the word free, think about Christ and why he was the only perfect man to walk the face of this earth. Not just the fact that he was the Son of God, but he was perfect in his actions while he was here on earth. What about him was so different from us? He was born of flesh and blood, just like everybody else born on this earth. The difference was he lived his life free and lived by the laws of God and not by the laws of man. He even broke some laws, or should I say traditions. He was a man whose heart was pure and no man could change his mind. He wasn't trying to make everybody happy, but he told the truth even if it meant people would hate him for it.

Gospel of Thomas
16 Jesus said, "Men think, perhaps, that it is peace which I have come to cast upon the world. They do not know it is dissension which I have come to cast upon the earth: fire, sword, and war. ..." (Gnosis.org/naghamm/gthlamb.html)

He was a danger to a civilized world because he spoke against some of society's way of life. He knew that no man had power over him except what was given to them from the father. He prayed to the Father and believed what was in his heart. He didn't try to make the world worse, but he spent every day of his life trying to make it better by giving people the truth. He spent his life trying to make mankind better and trying to teach us the way to live and how to love one another. He could have ridden a chariot and lived like a king on earth, but he walked everywhere he went and rode a donkey once. He lived off the land and was homeless. He didn't know what he would eat or when he would drink; he just trusted in God. He could have invented any of the things we have today, but he chose to keep his life simple and lived the way the Father intended man to live. He was a carpenter, an occupation in which you learn to build things yourself and are not dependent on the world. He loved everyone around him, even if he knew they were bad and unjust. I mean, he hated their sin, but he still loved those people and tried to teach them a better way. He just prayed more for the people who hated and persecuted him for giving the world the truth. Christ taught us to love no matter what, because there is no joy in hating one another, as it says in the Bible.

> **Luke 6: 27–28**
> [27] *But I tell you who hear me: Love your enemies, do good to those who hate you,*
> [28] *bless those who curse you, and pray for them which despitefully use you.*

I took a deep breath during our conversation in the hood. I looked up at PJ and noticed he was crying. I knew at that moment exactly what he was crying for. It was because of the way his life was going. It was the same reason I wanted to cry, because life was hard, and maybe we realized it was only like that because we were doing it to ourselves, that it really wasn't our fault; it was the only thing we knew, but now that we knew different, we could choose to rise up and take claim over our lives. Civilization has brainwashed people out of living life free by telling them they are living like savages. I would rather be called a savage and live free than be controlled and enslaved by a civilized world where I can no longer do what I want or think or speak freely.

After that night, I felt like I had a choice to make: was I to keep living the way I was living or would I serve the Lord; was I to take what I had learned and start a different life or was I to keep doing the same thing I have always been doing? I tried changing, and I did for about a day or two. I guess you could say I was a product of my environment, but ever since that night, I thought about writing a book, and something changed inside of me. So I prayed about it and God answered: knowing the outcome of writing this book, I knew one day I would have to make a choice. I started putting everything in my life together, and I opened my heart to the good in everything. I had thought about my dreams, the conversation with PJ and my friends, my life, and what was going on in the world. After doing some research and praying, I started to understand the beginning, the present, and what I know will be the fate of the world if we don't change. After I started to live my life free, I realized I was blessed, and so I accepted the task of writing this book. Once I did, it was almost like God placed everything that I needed to know in front of me. Eventually, I changed, with the help of prayer and faith. I had made up my mind, and although I didn't always show it, I was free in my heart and my mind and poor in spirit, and I loved God and everybody around me. I was in love with life, though sometimes I couldn't help the things that had been programmed into my mind. It's a day to day work in progress, and some bad habits and addictions in my life have taken time to break. I don't pretend to be perfect; I just live to be real. While on this journey, I realized that everything my eyes were opening up to was preparing me for the end, which is rapidly approaching. In my opinion, the meaning of life is simple: love and live life free.

CHAPTER 4

FREE LOVE

Life is precious and beautiful, and the best part about life is love. Some people spend a lifetime searching for it. When I looked up the definition of love, it said that it was "a proudly tender, passionate affection for another person or a feeling of warm personal attachment of deep affection as a parent, a friend, or child." In my opinion, when you love someone, your whole life changes, not for the worse, but for the better. It means communicating with each other and understanding each other's needs and wants. It means you would put that person before yourself and make sacrifices for them. That means accepting and loving that person for their flaws and all, and sometimes, when you love someone, their flaws become the very thing you love most about them. Love isn't about finding a perfect person. It's about seeing an imperfect person perfectly. It doesn't mean you try to change the person you are with, but that you try to change yourself to be better for the person you love and accept them for who they are. Praying for them and appreciating every moment spent with them. Sharing your life and dreams with the one you love, and not just part of your dreams, but all of them. Giving your all and not being afraid to love them completely and unconditionally. It means being dedicated, honest, respectful, romantic at times, and loyal, never keeping secrets from each other. There is no such thing as privacy in a relationship or in a marriage. Why hide anything from the person you love, because if you truly love them, what would you have to hide? Getting married and loving your partner in sickness and in health until death do you part. Having known love, I can tell you there is no greater feeling or emotion. I have seen and felt love at its highest and at its lowest. I have witnessed pure happiness and I have endured love's harsh pain when it is lost.

I, myself, have been in love twice before. One you've heard about, Turtle, and the other I love to this day. She's beautiful, kind-hearted, God fearing, and not moved by money. That's something that's rare in my book. The problem was that I fell in love with a woman who was in love with someone else. When I met her, she had just broken up with her ex-boyfriend two months prior to meeting me and still wasn't over him. We had so much fun together and she laughed at all my jokes. We talked every day, all day on the phone for a year straight. She was like my best friend and something more. I tried to hold back the fact that I really wanted to be in a relationship, because she was scared of the very word, and after how her last boyfriend did her, I guess I really couldn't blame her. Even though we talked like we were together, even though we kissed like we were together, and even though we sometimes told each other "I love you," I still couldn't call her mine. Every time I took a step forward, she took two steps back, trying to protect her already broken heart. I didn't know what to do to gain her trust or how I could make her see how much I really loved her. I just knew that I wouldn't stop trying to prove to her that the love I had for her was real. We had been dating a year and a half, and that was longer than the longest relationship I had had, which was with Turtle. Turtle and I were together for a little over a year, until we broke up. To be honest, after Turtle, it took me a long time to find someone who believed in love like I did and who was a genuinely good person. When I found her, it seemed like what I had been looking for was so close but yet so far away. It's like being given the best gift you can ask for but never being able to open it and having to look at it every day.

After I felt like she had finally got over her past relationship, the moment I felt like she could actually be ready for a relationship and we had a shot at being together, I couldn't write or think clear anymore, because all I could think about was her. Even though she was one of my biggest inspirations, she would be one of my biggest setbacks. She made me want to be better as a person, but when it came time for me to clear my mind to write, I couldn't. Everything I needed was in my mind, but I couldn't put it on paper.

Before I started writing this book, I prayed, and while in prayer, the Lord told me that if I chose to write this book, it wouldn't be an easy road, but to trust him. He told me that he would begin to take the distractions out of my life if I started to procrastinate, and that it wasn't to punish me, but so that I would finish the task he entrusted to me on time. He took most of my clothes away in the fire at my mother's. He took my car away while I was driving on the freeway after helping a friend. He took my son away to live with his mother in Atlanta. He took my finances away to ensure that I wouldn't go out. He left me with enough to pay my phone bill at times and to buy food. He took the TV in the house I stayed in away, along with that other roommate we used to have. He made me completely dependent on him for whatever came my way. When I saw my love as a distraction, I started to panic, because I knew that he would take her away too. She started calling a little less and I took it as evidence he was taking her away from me, and even though we weren't together, besides my son, she was one of the best things that ever happened to my life. So like a person afraid of losing love, I made the same mistake I made with Turtle. I managed to make her mad at me, but not enough that she would hate me, just enough so she would have a reason not to call or answer my calls for a while. I wanted to tell her the truth, but I didn't want her to feel like she was holding me back from doing something I felt I was born to do.

So I did and do what I have to until it is done and can only hope that through everything, her love for me will be enough for her to forgive me and maybe one day give me another chance. If not, then I can only hope she finds someone that loves her as much as I do. Maybe one day we can be together, because we can't choose who we love, and I can't help loving her, and if we can't be together, I only hope to gain her friendship back. Now that I know her, I can't imagine her not being a part of my life. In this day and time, real love is hard to find and hold together through all the things that come with love.

Things just aren't the way they used to be; they've changed over the course of history. Love hasn't changed just the way we live has changed, and that's the part that makes love so darn hard. Not just in relationships, but as families and with all mankind, it seems as though love is lost. It's almost like we are distracted by everything except for the things that matter. When I look at the world, love is not the first thing that comes to mind, but it should be.

> **1 John 4:7–8**
> *⁷ Beloved, let us love one another: for love is of God; and every one that loveth is born of God, and knoweth God.*
> *⁸ He that loveth not knoweth not God; for God is love.*

I mean, let's just look back through history. The closer we get to today's date, the shorter amount of time relationships and marriages last, the more people have lost family values and love for each other. I believe there is a reason behind the lost love. See, the further we look back, the easier it seems to have been to find companionship. It was easier to be a family and easier for people to help their fellow man. We didn't have as many distractions, communication wasn't this advanced, and temptation was a lot less. The world changed and we unknowingly let it change us, and not in a good way.

In earlier times, a man and a woman played different roles in their family. It was similar to, yet different from what it is today.

Everything they did every day revolved around family teaching, learning, and spending time with each other. A man's job was to hunt and fish to get meat to cook for his family. They made their own clothes to wear every day. They built their own houses and taught their sons how to build for their families and to provide shelter. They used to make things to trade with other people to get what they needed. A woman's job was to gather water, fruits, and vegetables for meals for her family. To cook, clean, take care of the home, and nurture her children. The parents were the first people to love a child at birth, and they were their teachers. They taught their children everything until the day they became adults and they were to be on their own. They raised their children and molded them into being the adults they became.

Proverbs 22:6
6 Train up a child in the way he should go: and when he is old, he will not depart from it.

They looked at their children as another blessing and not another bill or mouth to feed. They were taught to do everything themselves and not to depend on anyone else, and if they didn't have things, they traded for them. Families spent time together, they had all the time in the world, and things were simple. They learned more than anything about the value of having a family and being there for one another. They were still happy without all the things that we have today, and it was less complicated, so they were less stressed about life. The simpler things are in a relationship, the longer it allows you to be together. I'm talking about a time when love was free and families were able to live and love without the stress of bills, buying food, paying rent, or any other cost that comes with living a day in this day and time.

Romans 13:8
8 Owe no man anything, but to love one another: for he that loveth another hath fulfilled the law.

It was a time when money wasn't the most important thing that people thought about, and they just cared about providing for their families. It didn't matter how rich or poor a person was, and love was all you needed. Sin has always been a part of life after the first sin was committed, but either people sinned and tried to hide it, they were forced to sin, deceived into sinning, or they were too powerful for people to go against their sins.

Nowadays, people sin openly and barely care about their sins. We live in a world where wrong seems right and bad seems good, and the good are treated like outcasts. People rationalize about things they know are wrong to try to make them right. The world is so corrupt, most people believe the only way to survive and make it is by showing no love and doing wrong. Nowadays, things are completely different. The mindsets of men and women have completely changed. We barely ever spend time with our parents now. Parents are still the first to love us at birth and we still learn everything from them. That is, up until we are old enough to go to school or daycare. Then we spend our time learning from complete strangers for most of our lives, when we should be learning from the people who love us the most, our beloved family. Instead, we are treated like robots, forced to download information until we gain a skill. I mean, think about what I am saying: we go to school eight hours a day, not to mention the time we spend getting to and from school. Then we get home and have an hour or more worth of homework to do. Then children want to go outside and spend time with friends, and that's only if a child is into that. The average child in America isn't into going outside to play with friends. Children have all new ways of having fun, like watching their favorite shows on TV, surfing the web, listening to the radio, playing video games, and anything else they like to spend their time doing. They might be lucky to spend a day with their parents, and then when they do, they hate it, because they're not used to it. None of their friends have parents like that, and before you know it, they've grown up and it's too late for the parents to teach them anything. They feel like they've grown out of that stage in their life, like it's too late to tell them anything because they're old enough to make their own decisions. The average interactive time children spend with their parents once they've started school is probably two hours a day or less. Even less time if the parents don't work the same time their children are at school.

Whoever said that entertainment media doesn't have an influence on a person's life must not have realized how much time we spend watching and listening to those things. At school the main thing students talk to their friends about every day is what was on TV, video games, and what happened on a social network the night before. We spend way more time with entertainment and school than we do with our families. The only thing we are really always taught and that is programmed into our minds by society and our parents is to go to school to be somebody and make money. I'm sure that gives people the feeling that if they don't have money, they're a failure. That they're not somebody in this world, they're nobody. It causes them to become somewhat insecure about who they are, because society starts to pay attention to what they have instead of who they are. That's probably why there are so many deadbeat parents; either they have no family values, or they weren't raised in a loving family environment. Some people are addicted to the lifestyle they live without kids and responsibility. They're afraid they won't have enough money to support their families and leave without trying. Society and technology really takes away from families being families. I can't tell you the last time I heard about a family sitting and eating dinner together at a dinner table, but it was probably a holiday.

The world has changed. You really don't see kids playing outside, exploring things, or having fun anymore. Growing up now, we are never really taught how to love, how to be a family, or how to treat our mates. We can only go by the things we see or hear. When we are taught to love, we are taught to only love certain people, to keep our circle of friends small, and no matter whom we love, to never trust them completely. Sometimes we are taught never to trust our mates and never to get married. That we should show no love, because love will get us killed. Well, if God is love, then showing love is something I would gladly give my life for. So the next time you hear about a child, teenager, or young adult not showing love, doing wrong by his mate or parents, or doing wrong in the world, just think about the fact that the life you see them living may be the only life they have ever known. The world may be the only family they have ever known, and nobody has taught them any better or any other way. You, the people around them, or this so-called civilized world we live in may have taught them to be the way they are. If you want to find somebody to blame, look in a mirror, because we are the people allowing it to happen.

As far as relationships go nowadays, by the time we reach our teenage years, the stress of failed love or struggling to pay bills has already set in on our parents. Even if they weren't stressed about bills and paid everything on time, nowadays men and women are taught the same things: that a relationship won't last without money and that they need it to love someone. I'm sure you're reading this part thinking, nothing is free in this world, including love, but I believe a person can be completely happy without money being a factor, as long as he can survive and have found peace. Like me, for example, I don't have a lot of things that I have been programmed to believe I need, and I couldn't be happier.

There are so many reasons why relationships don't work, but one of the biggest reasons I believe they fail is because most people want love but are afraid of it. Love can make you happy, sad, a number of different emotions, but it is the pain when it's lost that causes people not to have faith in or believe in love. It's not the thought that we will never find it, but that when we do, our mates might be faced with temptation and opportunity. It causes people to lose faith in love, it makes us afraid of giving our all in a relationship or marriage, and it creates a fear of getting hurt. It is that fear of getting hurt that causes us to put up that wall, never really letting someone in and never treating our mates the way they should be treated. Some people even cheat, thinking that their mates could be doing the same thing, that if they do it first, it will somehow lessen the pain if love is lost or they catch their companions cheating. When people put up that wall in order to protect themselves from being hurt, it often unknowingly changes their character. They hide behind a fake personality they've created instead of being themselves. In today's world, I don't believe that most people even know who they really are because of the change in character or the need to be the people they think other people want them to be. The change in character causes us to be less satisfying and fulfilling to our partners and makes them more likely to cheat and fall victim to the very thing we feared. Also, it makes some people open to homosexuality to gain the things they need and look for in their partner.

In my observations, most men hide behind money and are afraid to be a one-woman man. They somehow develop the need to act like they don't care and like it will be easy to move on. When, actually, they do care and never really realize how much they really do love and care about a woman until she's gone. Most women pretend to be money hungry, and they start to act and think like men so they won't get hurt. In the end, they're really just going to hurt themselves, because their men will leave them anyway. No man really wants a woman that thinks like a man. What's wrong with thinking like a woman? When it comes to love, money should never be the reason it didn't work, because love doesn't cost a thing. There are too many factors to why love is now complicated when it should be so simple. The temptation part of it is caused by the fact that in society, sex sells, not to mention that we have drugs and alcohol that sometimes add to the temptation. In these days, we are living in a very sexual society, which believes the more sexually open you are, the more sex appeal you have, and the more attractive and popular you are. Most people feel as though the more skin you show or the tighter your clothing is, the more people can see your curves. There are very few people who leave anything to the imagination anymore. They use these sexy methods to attract the interest of their audiences, whoever they may be. The only problem is that they get everyone's attention, even the interest of people involved with others. With all the temptation out there today, it's only a matter of time until the opportunity presents itself for someone to cheat.

Technology has improved a great deal over the years and it has created more ways to communicate. There are cell phones, computers, video chatting, social networks, dating sites, and many other ways to communicate or have social meetings. It is the thought that your mate may be tempted through those things or by the persuasion of other people around them, either with technology or in the world, that makes most people develop trust issues in their relationships. If you can't trust someone, how can you truly love them? How can you truly give yourself and your all to the person you love? When it comes to communicating with others, everyone wants privacy from their partners. I personally don't believe in privacy on either side of a relationship. My grandparents don't need privacy; they share everything together. They have even shared the same phone for the last thirty years. They don't have secrets between each other and it makes it easier for them to trust each other, I think.

When it comes to the people around you, not just family, but friends, the people you know and interact with every day, and even strangers, you should always treat them with love and kindness. You should want to help any of these people when they're in need without expecting anything in return. Christ gives us two commandments: he says, first, to love God and, second, to love one another.

John 15:9–15

9 As the Father hath loved me, so have I loved you: continue ye in my love.

10 If ye keep my commandments, ye shall abide in my

love; even as I have kept my Father's commandments, and abide in his love.

¹¹ These things have I spoken unto you, that my joy might remain in you, and that your joy might be full.

¹² This is my commandment, That ye love one another, as I have loved you.

¹³ Greater love hath no man than this, that a man lay down his life for his friends.

¹⁴ Ye are my friends, if ye do whatsoever I command you.

¹⁵ Henceforth I call you not servants; for the servant knoweth not what his lord doeth: but I have called you friends; for all things that I have heard of my Father I have made known unto you.

God gives us strength to help others, which is why we should be trying to help someone else every day. What would it hurt to do random acts of kindness and good deeds? I don't know how we got to the point where we are so selfish, but if you love God, you would want to help anyone you could with no thought of yourself. I always hear people saying they are too nice, but if you love God, there is no such thing. When you look at some elderly with all their wisdom, they can't stand to see someone in need of help and they help and give there last to help anyone in any way they can. I always say people who love money more than they love people will turn on you in a minute. One reason I believe it's going to be so hard for rich people to get to heaven is because some of them have sold their souls to get their fame and riches. Another reason is because money changes people. You can say it doesn't, but it does; I know from experience. When you become obsessed with money, gaining wealth, and material things, you lose your humanity and greed takes over. I don't see how anyone can say they love God and then stand by watching people suffer in poverty in a society run by money. They have the power to help but don't.

1 John 3:17
¹⁷ But whoso hath this world's good, and seeth his brother have need, and shutteth up his bowels of compassion from him, how dwelleth the love of God in him?

I don't see how anyone can watch a person struggle, suffer, or be in pain and not feel anything that's not love. You want to know what love is:

1 Corinthians 13:4–8
⁴ Love is patient, love is kind. It does not envy, it does not boast, it is not proud.
⁵ It does not dishonor others, it is not self-seeking, it is not easily angered, it keeps no record of wrongs.
⁶ Love does not delight in evil but rejoices with the truth.
⁷ It always protects, always trusts, always hopes, always perseveres.
⁸ Love never fails.

As long as there are poor people in the world, I will never be rich and I will give and do for the poor as much as I can until the day I am in heaven with my savior and friend, Christ, and my Heavenly Father, God.

Proverbs 22:9
⁹ He that hath a bountiful eye shall be blessed; for he giveth of his bread to the poor.

If you're reading this, even though I may never have the pleasure of meeting you, I want you to know that it doesn't matter who you are or where you're from, I love you and there is nothing you can do about it.

The change in character happens because of the fear of losing love or because people have been hurt before is, I think, the main reasons for people being so open to homosexuality today. The change and pain mixed with a little curiosity and the ease of communication is what I believe has caused more people to become homosexual. There are some who, since childhood, have felt out of place and have always been attracted to someone of the same sex, or curious as to how it would be to be with someone of the same sex. They even feel like they were born the wrong sex and they were supposed to be the opposite sex. In that case, I think that it was just a personal decision to be homosexual that developed from that person's childhood years and that it was not so much influenced by the world around them. It has always been in some people's minds that they are homosexual, and that just may be who they are; nobody is the same, everybody is different. The other reasons I believe people become homosexual are because they're a freak, they're searching for something to be a part of to fill an emptiness in their lives, or they're a follower. From what I have observed over the years, most men and women are overcome with homosexual curiosity because of porn. In the privacy of their own homes, people watch whatever form of porn they want. When they get tired of watching the form of erotica they often look at, they start to venture off the usual. Once they get into watching it, they wonder what it would feel like to actually commit the act.

Some women do it because they have heard how great the experience is through friends, social networks, or the media. They also know that most men are attracted to it and rather enjoy the thought of two women being together sexually. The thought of having two women at once has even crossed my mind a few times in my life. Sometimes it's because women have heard sex is better with another woman, and men just haven't pleased them in the right way sexually. They feel as though a woman could do it better, because some men don't have emotional sex or participate in foreplay because of the change in their character. I also feel that a good majority of people become homosexual because they're searching for a characteristic or emotion from their partner that never shows. It doesn't show because of the change due to the fear of rejection or fear of being hurt, whether it is in sexual activities, being romantic, listening to each other's needs, wanting to be held, or whatever it may be. Nowadays, people are so sexually open to trying new things that after sleeping with so many people of the opposite sex, they get bored and start to try new things. What surprised me the most was to find out that a lot of the people I went to school with, grew up with, or hung around with have done something with someone of the same sex, male and female. I can only tell you the things I have observed from them and their lives on the subject of homosexuality. I hope I don't offend any man or woman for being homosexual or being attracted to the same sex. What you do with your life is what you do, it's your choice.

You can't look down on anyone for wanting love and searching for the characteristics needed in a mate to be happy. You can't judge people on the things they want to do, because no one is without sin. God gave everyone freewill. All I can do is show you what the Bible says about these things and give my personal opinion on the matter. After all, this book is about my thoughts. I just hope that you respect me for being honest and truthful.

Leviticus 20:13
13 And if a man also lie with mankind, as he lieth with a woman, both of them have committed an abomination, they shall surely be put to death; their blood shall be upon them.

I feel that homosexuality is wrong, especially since during my studies I learned that one of the initiation rituals to the most powerful satanic occult organization in the world is committing a homosexual act. In my opinion, if God meant for two people of the same sex to be together, he would have given everyone the same body parts. Instead, he made a man and a woman like two puzzle pieces, connected by a man's penis and a woman's vagina. Homosexuality is like putting two positive pieces of a battery together and expecting a flashlight to come on; the light will never shine. I believe it is wrong in God's eyes to be homosexual and to be with someone of the same sex; therefore, I believe it is wrong. I am not saying that I dislike any homosexuals. I'm just saying I am not homosexual and I feel that it's wrong. It is just what I believe in my heart and everyone is entitled to their own opinion. All the people I know that are homosexual are either freaks, followers, or too scared to be themselves to the person they love, because they're afraid of getting hurt or judged. Which tells me we live in a society of lust and sexuality, people who are searching for acceptance and just following someone else's lead, and people too afraid to keep it real and take a chance on love. The fact is, most people are just doing it because it is now accepted in society and being promoted as a good thing, and they want to be accepted. Even though I feel homosexuality is wrong, I can't judge people who are or treat them differently. I can say this, though, as a message to everyone who is thinking about becoming homosexual or who is homosexual already. If you're going to be homosexual, or anything in life for that matter, make sure you're doing it because that's who you are and not because someone or something that happened influenced you to be something you are not.

In today's times, with everything that is happening in the world, it almost seems impossible to find a good person to settle down with.

> **Proverbs 18:22**
> *22 Whoso findeth a wife findeth a good thing, and obtaineth favour of the Lord.*

Most people in today's world value and are looking for the wrong things out of life. God gave us freewill and everyone is free to do whatever they like. I just feel that people shouldn't question God's creation; he made people who they are for a reason. I think the change in character has caused people to rationalize and feel okay to find love in places they also believe are wrong. I believe in this crazy world we live in, we are all capable of showing love and compassion to each other. Maybe if we open our hearts a little bit more and take a long, hard look in the mirror at who we really are and love ourselves, we can forgive those who wronged us in the past and maybe begin to trust in our mates completely and give real love a chance. We can pay more attention to our children and teach them something the world has failed to teach: what's right. We can stop depending on money to solve everything and spend more time with our families and get to know, love, and cherish the person we're with and the people we are around. We can begin to love life and the people around us as God loves us. I am talking about free, unconditional love.

CHAPTER 5

THE BEGINNING OF THE END

"In the beginning, God created the heavens and the earth." Most people believe that you have to make it to heaven to live in paradise. They have never thought about the fact that God created both the heavens and the earth. That, like heaven, the world we live in today was also created as a paradise in the beginning. I mean, after really looking into the story of Adam and Eve and the way Christ lived, you understand that living the way they lived is the only way to the kingdom of heaven. The only way man can live without sin is by living free, having faith, completely depending on and loving God, and loving other people.

Before I explain to you why the world is about to end and why it is the way it is today, what is now happening, and what we are in store for in the future, I must first explain to you what happened in the beginning, what changed us, because in the beginning, there is the end.

Gospel of Thomas
[18] The disciples said to Jesus, "Tell us how our end will be." Jesus said, "Have you discovered, then, the beginning, that you look for the end? For where the beginning is, there will the end be. Blessed is he who will take his place in the

THE BEGINNING OF THE END

beginning: he will know the end and will not experience death." (Gnosis.org/naghamm/gthlamb.html)

We know in the beginning Adam and Eve committed and brought about sin by disobeying God. We also know that it was a serpent that tricked them into eating the forbidden fruit. We also know from the Bible that fallen angels liked, slept with, and had offspring with the women of earth. We also know from the Bible that fallen angels convinced mankind into being sinners, so God destroyed the earth with a flood. What we don't know are the details and specifics. The Bible paints a great picture, but to me, it's one that is incomplete. When I really thought about it, everything about history was incomplete. That is, until I started piecing the stories together, and after studying a little bit of history, it all started to make sense. I realized that earlier civilizations recorded similar stories of the events that took place in the beginning. Although, their stories on what happened are slightly different and more detailed. They not only recorded the arrival of fallen angels, but they also recorded what it was the fallen angels taught mankind. The stories they told left us clues about why the world is the way it is today.

Now that I look at this world, everything that we do today that makes society controlled, greedy, unequal, advanced, and dependent on man came from what the fallen angels taught mankind when they once walked the earth. The world has been set up to be this way since the beginning. They deceived us, and now the world is controlled by those who follow what fallen angels left behind. It is my belief that when Lucifer and the rest of the fallen angels were cast out of heaven, they visited many civilizations all across the world. They deceived and convinced the people of those times to leave behind information for a more advanced, organized, and civilized society to follow. What they did was just the beginning to the end of man. What I am about to tell you from this point on in this book will be very disturbing. No matter what you believe in, all I ask is that you finish this book, because knowing the truth may save your life.

Before the Fallen Angels were cast out of heaven, a war broke out. Lucifer was defeated. He, along with a third of the angels in heaven, were cast out of heaven and down upon the earth.

> **Revelations 12:1-17**
> *¹ And there appeared a great wonder in heaven; a woman clothed with the sun, and the moon under her feet, and upon her head a crown of twelve stars:*
>
> *² And she being with child cried, travailing in birth, and pained to be delivered*
>
> *³ And there appeared another wonder in heaven; and behold a great red dragon, having seven heads and ten horns, and seven crowns upon his heads.*
>
> *⁴ And his tail drew the third part of the stars of heaven, and did cast them to the earth: and the dragon stood before the woman which was ready to be delivered, for to devour her child as soon as it was born.*
>
> *⁵ And she brought forth a man child, who was to rule all nations with a rod of iron: and her child was caught up unto God, and to his throne.*
>
> *⁶ And the woman fled into the wilderness, where she hath a place prepared of God, that they should feed her there a thousand two hundred and threescore days.*
>
> *⁷ And there was war in heaven: Michael and his angels fought against the dragon; and the dragon fought and his angels,*
>
> *⁸ And prevailed not; neither was their place found anymore in heaven.*
>
> *⁹ And the great dragon was cast out, that old serpent, called the Devil, and Satan which deceiveth the whole world, he was cast out into the earth, and his angels were cast out with him.*

> ¹⁰ And I heard a loud voice saying in heaven, Now is come salvation, and strength, and the kingdom of our God, and the power of his Christ: for the accuser of our brethren I cast down, which accused them before our God day and night.
>
> ¹¹ And they overcame him by the blood of the Lamb, and by the word of their testimony; and they loved not their lives unto the death.
>
> ¹² Therefore rejoice, ye heavens, and ye that dwell in them. Woe to the inhabiters of the earth and of the sea! For the devil has come down unto you, having great wrath, because he knoweth that he hath but a short time.
>
> ¹³ And when the dragon saw that he was cast unto the earth, he persecuted the woman which brought forth the man child.
>
> ¹⁴ And to the woman were given two wings of a great eagle, that she might fly into the wilderness, into her place, where she is nourished for a time, and times, and a half a time, from the face of the serpent.
>
> ¹⁵ And the serpent cast out of his mouth water as a flood after the woman, that he might cause her to be carried away of the flood.
>
> ¹⁶ And the earth helped the woman, and the earth opened her mouth, and swallowed up the flood which the dragon cast out of his mouth.
>
> ¹⁷ And the dragon was wroth with the woman, and went to make war with the remnant of her seed, which keep the commandments of God, and have the testimony of Jesus Christ.

There are a lot of very important things to pay attention to in this passage. The first thing to understand is that when Lucifer was cast down to earth, he knew that he only had a little time before he would be locked away in the bottomless pit. That means he only had a little time to teach man, because in order to deceive the world, you have to teach the world. He came to do a job, to deceive the whole world, and from what I know about this world, he succeeded. He instilled beliefs in man that would change us and slowly ensure that the world would believe in and follow his philosophy. Lucifer's philosophy is that anyone can become a god. That is, if they follow his teachings, submit to his will, and worship him. Those who follow Lucifer's teachings believe that those who don't will be slaves to those who do. The most important part of this passage is that even though the devil has set a trap, even though the world has been deceived and we have been made slaves, we can all be set free of this through the testimony of Christ.

Satan was very clever and he used his knowledge and beauty to turn other angels against the one true God.

> **Ezekiel 28:17**
> *17 Thine heart was lifted up because of thy beauty, thou has corrupted thy wisdom by reason of thy brightness: I will cast thee to the ground, I will lay thee before kings, that they may behold thee.*

I believe God didn't destroy Lucifer or the other fallen angels because he didn't want his other angels to serve him out of fear, but out of love. God could have easily destroyed Satan after he rebelled against him in heaven, but God is kind, loving, and forgiving. God also knew that one day his son, the comforter, would come to lead us all to truth. He wanted to teach Satan a lesson. He allowed Lucifer to walk the earth and deceive man because he knew that one day we would realize the deception and lies and begin to walk in the spirit of truth, that we would one day stand united against evil, against all that he has done. That we would find the strength to change in the darkest of days and stand for all that is right.

When Lucifer was cast out of God's everlasting light and authority, he convinced other angels to turn against God. If Satan can convince angels to turn on God, those who have seen the Father, then why don't people believe it would be difficult to do the same to man? Lucifer gave the other angels the same offer that was given to Eve: a chance to be treated as a god under Lucifer's rule. Satan wanted to be able to make choices like God and to be worshipped by mankind as a god. So he convinced a third of the angels in heaven that they would be worshipped as gods by man. Then he convinced man that if they bowed to him, they, too, could become gods through the path of enlightenment. That through his knowledge, they could rule the world and one day take their places among gods. This war has always been about Lucifer's lust for power and his need to be worshipped by all. He would offer you the world just to gain your soul. God gave man the power of choice and freewill, and Lucifer tried to use that to his advantage. It is my belief that while the fallen angels walked the earth, they taught, directed, and deceived us into being who we are today.

Now, I know what I am telling you is a bit much, but it is the truth, and to prove it, let's take a trip down history so you can better understand. The Bible talks about the fallen angels and how they lived here on earth. It talks about what they did after being cast out of heaven, but it is my belief that the very first civilization to be able to read and write left behind a detailed record of their arrival. The Sumerians, who are considered by many the oldest advanced civilization known to man, have similar views of the fallen angels; you see, like the Bible, they recorded a group of beings coming from the sky. They believed in and called these creatures that fell from the heavens the Anunnaki. The word Anunnaki means "those from heaven to earth came." The Anunnaki were said to be a reptilian race and were known to the Sumerians as the creators of life. Some people nowadays even call them engineers, convinced that these creatures somehow engineered or altered man's DNA. What do the Anunnaki and the fallen angels in the Bible have in common? They were all described throughout history as looking like humans, having wings, and being giant or very tall. The skeletons of these giants have been discovered in regions all across the world.

Not only does the Bible talk about these beings, but there is no doubt that earlier civilizations believed that these beings once walked the earth. When they arrived, they convinced man that they were gods and that they should worship them instead of the one true God. I mean, think about it, if you were an angel and you were cast out of heaven for rebelling against God, would you present yourself as an angel, a servant to the one true God you're rebelling against, or would you present yourself as a god? Make up a lie about why you're there and trick God's children into serving you and not him by pretending to be the creator? Man, being deceived, began to praise and worship these creatures that fell from the sky as gods.

After lying and convincing man that they were gods. They told yet another lie about being cast out of heaven. They couldn't tell the Sumerians or any other civilization they were cast out of heaven, because man would have rejected them. They would have been viewed as the bad guys. They couldn't tell people they were angels, because that would acknowledge the one true God's power. So they told the Sumerians that they were there because their planet was dying, that the only way they could save their dying planet was with gold. That made ancient civilizations believe that gold was the element of the gods. They made the Sumerians mine for gold to give to them as offerings. In today's world, every Luciferian on earth controls, owns, and buys the world's gold. It's because of their gods that gold is so important to them. That's the real reason they started printing paper money and started trading and buying up all the world's gold. They needed to collect and gain control of it. They gained the world's gold, and in return, they offered the world paper worth nothing or credit, which is money that never existed. They have mastered all kinds of ways to gain gold. In today's world, the ones who own the gold control and make the rules. They live above the law like gods, controlling the outcome of all major decisions. We know that the Sumerians offered the Annunaki gold to please them. That kind of makes me wonder why we have all these commercials on TV asking to buy our gold. I mean, are those believers in Lucifer preparing to make an offering of gold in the near future? Gold controls the world now, and since the arrival of the Annunaki, it has always been important to every civilized society throughout history.

Once they convinced man that they were gods and that the only reason they were there was because they needed gold to save their planet, the next thing they did was start to teach man, helping them to advance. Making sure that man advanced was a vital part to their plan being successful, and by the end of this chapter, you will understand why. When the Annunaki first arrived, they talked to everyone. They lived amongst the people, teaching them to be civilized, teaching them to be more advanced. Then, once the Sumerians started learning and had enough knowledge, Annunaki changed how everything was set up. They changed the whole structure of the Sumerian society. The Annunaki stopped living amongst the people and started to rule over them. They told the people they could no longer speak to them, that the only person who could speak directly to them was the person they appointed as the ruler, that the ruler they appointed was to be considered and worshipped as a living god because of his knowledge. That is why in those times people believed that whatever ruler governed over them was chosen by the gods. There have even been other documented accounts of those gods manifesting themselves in the leaders of different civilizations. I believe that rituals and planetary alignments may have something to do with these so-called gods manifesting themselves into people. Nevertheless, gods manifesting themselves in the rulers almost sounds like demonic possession. All I know is they lived amongst us and helped us grow. They filled us with knowledge to help us advance. They told us gold was the world's most precise resource. Then they appointed someone ruler and made him a living god. Then the ruler appointed people under him to carry out his orders. When you put all of those facts together, you see how Lucifer architecturally designed the world we live in today. He deceived us and now we live a civilized lie every day.

The gold also caused man to be greedy. The more gold a person had, the bigger his offering was to the so-called gods. The bigger the offering a person had, the more praised and higher up in society he was. That, along with appointing one man to rule over the others and then that man appointing people of power under him, was the birth of civilized times. It also was the first time man became unequal. Being unequal gives way to people being treated differently, some almost godlike for what they have, and others like nothing for what they don't. The poor began to be treated badly and the rich with the utmost respect. Man began being judged by what they had instead of who they were. In an unequal society, when you start to believe someone is above you, you start to listen to what they have to say and start to follow their teachings and what they believe. They become role models and you look up to them because they have accomplished what you dream of doing. The inequality of man also created something I like to call the pyramid effect. Meaning, one person is at the top of the pyramid, whether he is known or unknown to society. He controls a group of people under him and they do whatever he says. Then they teach whatever he teaches them to whomever is under them. Then each of them teaches their own group of people, and so on and so on. This method is used as a tool to keep control over the people. Everything on earth is controlled by this method, even the church. We are all equal; no man should have authority over another, but because of what happened in the beginning, we are all treated differently instead of as equals. We see that more today than we ever have in the past.

Both in the book of Genesis and in the history of the Anunnaki, it is said that the fallen angels liked human women and took them as wives and slept with them. It was because of the mixed breeding and because, like the fallen angels, the hearts of man turned evil through the teachings of Lucifer that God destroyed mankind on earth. God sent a flood because of the continuous evil in the hearts of man; it is the story of Noah's Ark.

Genesis 6:2–5

² That the sons of God saw the daughters of men that they were fair; and they took them wives of all which they chose.

³ And the Lord said, My spirit shall not always strive with man, for that he also is flesh: yet his days shall be an hundred and twenty years.

⁴ There were giants in the earth in those days; and also after that, when the sons of God came in unto the daughters of men, and they bare children to them, the same became mighty men which were of old, men of renown.

⁵ And God saw that the wickedness of man was great in the earth, and that every imagination of the thoughts of his heart was only evil continually.

When God destroyed the earth the first time, it is said that all the fallen angels, with the exception of Lucifer, were locked away. That the offspring of the fallen angels were destroyed, but since they were half-man, half-angel, the part of each that was an angel turned into a spirit. Those spirits are now known as demons and evil spirits.

My question about history is, when did the great flood actually happen and how big was the world to the civilization that described the great flood? During my research, I realized that every one of these ancient societies that were visited by these so-called gods dramatically failed or disappeared. It's almost like they disappeared without a trace or explanation as to what happened. Because of the way things were placed in those cities, it's almost like they disappeared overnight. Every civilization Lucifer visited was destroyed in some way shortly after he left and the people became evil. If the great flood is what caused the disappearance of the fallen angels, it had to have happened after they spread out across the world. It could not have been before all of these different ancient civilizations recorded fallen angels, many gods, different gods, pagan gods, star people, ancient aliens, or whatever they were called when they were physically living here on earth amongst the people in those times. The first advanced civilization documented a race of giants falling from the heavens and praised them all as gods. That made me pay attention to other civilizations, and I realized that the Sumerians recognized more than one god, but they weren't the only civilization that did. I found that not only do the Mayans, Incas, Aztecs, Egyptians, Greeks, Babylonians, and the Hopi Indians praise more than one god, but their gods all have similarities to each other, just different names. All of the angels that were cast out of heaven could not pretend to be the God of life; nobody would have believed them. So they all chose something to be the god of so that people would believe in them. People then prayed to the god of whatever these beings claimed to be the god of. The question I asked myself is why it turned from many gods physically living here and being with different civilizations to one god physically being with each different civilization across the world, but all having the same principles, though slightly different beliefs on how mankind should be. Then to one god visiting different civilizations but being recognized as the most important god.

Through hieroglyphs we know that these so-called gods stayed together with for-sure three civilizations: the Sumerians, the Babylonians, and the Egyptians. It seems to me that after ancient Egyptians recorded many gods physically being here, it's almost like every other civilization just recorded knowing that there were many gods. The people praised them but never physically witnessed the gods being there together. I believe sometime after influencing and teaching Egyptians, the fallen angels spread out all across different regions of the world. After man tried to build the Tower of Babel which was a tower man tried to build up to the heavens, God made all the people separate all over the world and speak different languages. The Tower of Babel represented man trying to become equal to God and they were punished for it. So with man now being all over the world, the fallen split up to each rule over their own group of people, each to rule their own kingdom the way they saw fit but with the same basic principles of being civilized, controlled, and under the Luciferianism philosophy. That is why we have so many different religions and so many different cultures praising different gods around the world. I mean, sure all those gods seemed good and divine; they come from the Father, they were once in the light. They would always teach each place they ruled over some good. All religion has the same principles on how to be a good person. They did that so that it would seem right and as if they were of the light and the true God. The catch is they would always teach civilizations something evil or of darkness. Why teach man to commit evil acts when you have already convinced them you were a god? It is because whatever act they told people to do symbolized man's worship and submission to their power, their rule, and their rebellion against the one true God. They created the word "religion" to separate us as a way of control so we would never understand we are all one.

The thing that gives away that these pagan gods spread out is the different temples and pyramids built all around the world. I believe through temples, pyramids, and hieroglyphs, ancient civilizations may have left more information than we think they did, and I believe they are all somehow connected. Many of these ancient civilizations lived in different time periods, but created temples and pyramids with astronomical orientation, similar geometry, and mathematical precision, though they had absolutely no contact with each other. The temples and pyramids were built to have strategic orientation to the sun and to communicate with the heavens and the stars. These great monuments are similar in so many ways that it seems almost impossible for it to just be coincidence. There are just too many similarities between these megalithic sites to deny that they are somehow connected. It's almost like the same person or beings built them all around the world. For most of these sites there is still no explanation on how they were created and who really built them. No one can explain how people cut or moved the bricks and stones into place. They built temples and pyramids to last forever so that the information stored in them would last forever.

The fallen spread out, but their leader, Lucifer, could not be in all of those places at once. They spread out to cover more ground, making the world more civilized, more controlled, as Lucifer slowly made his rounds, teaching man his philosophy and giving them knowledge. He had to travel, deceive, and move on to the next place, and even then he couldn't get to everyone. That is why he wanted man to advance, because without technology, Lucifer couldn't possibly get worshipped by everyone on earth. Now all he has to do is perform a few false miracles and televise them, and then he is seen by the world. Another reason he wanted man to advance is because, over time, with the creation of technology, they would be too distracted to talk to, thank, and be dependent on God. Satan could use technology to slowly influence the world to do evil, so that through wealth and power, he could get people to influence the world and be worshipped like gods. I mean, just think about a celebrity, a president, or anyone with wealth, possessions, or material things. Now tell me they aren't worshipped like gods by the world today. They can't even walk outside without somebody screaming, wanting an autograph, or taking pictures of them. They are treated a whole lot differently. Those with a little wealth are treated like gods, but those with wealth and power behind the scenes believe they are gods to the people. They believe they should always control and govern over the people through the teachings of Lucifer. It is they who believe they can make any man a godlike figure if they pledge their allegiance to him. They took the knowledge the Fallen Angels left behind and used it to their advantage. It is possible that all of the fallen could have left information behind, but for the most part, the information people follow came from Lucifer himself. After the fallen angels spread out all over the world, something happened and they all disappeared and then only one remained.

Throughout ancient history, there were four gods that were

the most important of all of the pagan gods. The most common gods ancient civilizations worshipped are the sun god, the god of thunder, the feathered serpent god, and the dragon. I believe all three of those gods in history were the same pagan god. Lucifer was known as a serpent, a dragon, and a false god of light, and the god of thunder, because that describes how he fell from the sky in the Bible.

Luke 10:18
[18] And he said unto them, I beheld Satan as lightning fall from heaven.

The whole concept of there being many gods was because there were many angels that were cast out of heaven, but all of those angels answered to one. Those pagan gods spread out all over the world, and sometime before their disappearance, Lucifer began his journey. He traveled to many places, deceiving, lying, and spreading knowledge. Then he disappeared without a trace, and I believe the last civilization he may have visited was the Mayan people. The Mayans were the last group of people I heard of being visited by the feathered serpent god.

Even though Lucifer spread his influence and knowledge to different civilizations, the Sumerians were the first recorded civilization to witness these beings. They worshipped all of these so-called gods the same. Then I started to pay attention to the dollar bill and I started to wonder why they chose to put an Egyptian pyramid on the back with the all-seeing eye. It could be interpreted as suggesting that through the knowledge and teachings of Lucifer, men can become gods and control and govern over the people using the pyramid effect. It could also be because the man who gave them the key to understanding the knowledge of the fallen angels married an Egyptian woman and worshipped Egyptian gods. It is also a big possibility it is because of Amun Ra, or Amen Ra, that they chose to put an Egyptian pyramid on the back of the dollar, because it may have been the first time in history that Lucifer

(Amen Ra) was recognized as the god of all the other fallen angels. The all-seeing eye is also known as the Eye of Providence or the Eye of Horus, who is a part of Amen Ra. It is also known among some as the Eye of Lucifer. Any way you look at it, the pyramid is the foundation of the fallen angels' belief. They could not have control over everything without the pyramid effect; it would be almost impossible.

When dealing with Luciferians, you see symbols of Ancient Egypt everywhere. Ancient Egypt was the foundation of their learning and knowledge. That could be why man's first trip to the moon, Apollo 11, was coordinated by Dr. Farouk El-Baz, whose family just happens to be experts on Ancient Egypt. Maybe the study of Ancient Egypt is why we named our days of the week after pagan gods, like Sunday for "sun god" and Monday for "moon god." Maybe that's why we have a giant obelisk in the middle of our nation's capital or statues of ancient gods on every building in downtown Washington. Maybe it's the reason the Statue of Liberty doesn't look like a woman; it really is a statue of the sun god, or should I say Lucifer himself. We name after, celebrate, buy things with, and accept things that pay respect to pagan gods; some even have rituals to honor them.

It's not just the Freemasons, though, who have rituals or honor fallen angels in history. Most if not all fraternities, most gangs, secret societies, many organizations, and almost all of the world's religions honor ancient pagan gods, knowingly and unknowingly. Luciferians are enlightened to the real history of the world and believe they are chosen by the gods who once walked the earth. The Freemasons believe in protecting the knowledge that the fallen angels left behind through ancient civilizations. They have hidden codices so they can understand the language of the fallen. Those in power used the knowledge from the fallen angels to go forth conquering. Why doesn't the church acknowledge fallen angels actually physically being here, helping man to advance and giving them knowledge? It's because if you knew the truth, you would see they are successfully conquering us and that all the advancements we have today may have come from what fallen angels left behind. If you look at history, most of the great mathematicians and scientists were part of occult organizations or fraternities, and/or studied mystery religions. I'm not saying technology is evil, but it was taught to us for a purpose. I'm not saying we should go back to the Stone Age. I believe all of mankind is free to do what they want. I'm just saying, recognize why God said to "love not the world" and to walk in spirit.

> **1 John 2:15-16**
> ¹⁵ Love not the world, neither the things that are in the world. If any man love the world, the love of the Father is not in him.
> ¹⁶ For all that is in the world, the lust of the flesh, and the lust of the eyes, and the pride of life, is not of the Father, but is of the world.

God said this because the world is consumed and guided by evil; all things are created by God, but what if in the beginning he didn't want us to have this knowledge, because he knew it would lead to how we live today? What if it was Lucifer's intentions to make mankind play God and push the world into this lustful, greedy, seduced, and heartless direction it is moving? What if Lucifer counted on people in a civilized world to be power-driven? What if he knew that those in power would have the characteristics he needed for his organized plan to be carried out? What if his plan was to get everyone to live by his philosophy in a civilized world? He used our own freewill against us, because he knew God would let us make our own choices. God just wanted us to love. He wanted us to love and be dependent on him, to be dependent on ourselves, and to love each other, and if we have increased goods, to help somebody else less fortunate. He wanted us to be free, to teach our kids how to love, respect, and provide for their families.

Lucifer told Eve that if she ate the fruit, her eyes would be opened and she would be like a god. How do you make mankind feel or create acts like gods? Give him knowledge. I mean, just look at today's times: we can fly, go into space, even control the weather, change the climate, create earthquakes, clone people, engineer diseases, heal the sick, and take life at will. Picture if we had a time machine and jumped back in time. To ancient civilizations, we probably would have looked like gods with all the technology we have to do all the things we can in today's time. The other way you would make mankind like gods is to create different classes of people. Make a world where people are treated differently based on their wealth, material possessions, and power. We are all created equal, but we don't treat each other like we're equal. The fallen angels designed it so that the people with power could influence the world in the direction of the fallen. We have the poor, the middle class, the rich, and the rich and powerful. The rich and powerful are usually classified by those who own a large amount of the world's gold; they make the rules and they break the rules. They have controlled and influenced the world into this evil we currently live in. One generation after another raised to hate and feel no emotion. Lucifer not only tricked Adam and Eve into gaining knowledge of good and evil, he also stayed and taught mankind, making us smarter and pouring ideas into us to ensure we would always live a life of sin. That we would be dependent on science, math, astrology, and technology to live our everyday lives, instead of having faith and living every day completely dependent on God. We now live in an almost completely brainwashed civilization that believes we need things that we really don't need and have never needed to survive. We are so far from how God wanted us to live, and we have unknowingly been headed down a path created by fallen angels since the beginning of mankind.

My goal for this book is to expose the deception of this world and to reveal the truth to you the reader. I believe that when Christ was born, he was born not only to die for our sins, but to give testimony and stop the world from being deceived by Lucifer and the fallen angels. Without Adam and Eve biting the forbidden fruit, mankind wouldn't have knowledge of good or bad. Therefore, how can man stray away from the light if he has no knowledge of darkness? The problem nowadays is the world has become so corrupt, mankind can no longer tell the difference between the two, because the dark is being described and promoted as the light. We think too much and feel too little, we no longer show love, and we, more often than not, display our ability to ignore the troubling things going on around us.

Before you read the next part of this book, I would like for everyone to search the internet for something titled "The Secret Covenant of the Illuminati" and read it.

CHAPTER 6

AN ORGANIZED PLAN

The world has changed over time, and civilization has evolved over centuries into what we see today. A civilization with a hidden agenda that makes my mind often wonder in deep thought and sometimes question everything I have ever learned about history. A civilization designed with the purpose of controlling everything and everyone in the world. A world full of people who have been sitting in the dark for so long they are afraid of the light, because they have been distracted and blanketed with so many lies they don't even know they are slaves to a controlled system. A system that has been controlled by those who are power-driven and have secretly conquered and taken control of everything and made people helpless to what is coming. The power-driven have made us completely dependent on corporations owned by them, a justice system controlled by them, technology monitored by them, and an economy controlled and backed by them. I believe that the first step to the end of days was an organized plan to conquer and gain complete control or influence of the world's governments, politics, resources, religion, and people, whether that meant mentally or physically. I believe that the steps taken by those who desire to conquer mankind, gain power, and control of the earth are in fact the first seal John was talking about in the book of Revelations.

> **Revelation 6:1-2**
>
> ¹ *And I saw when the Lamb opened one of the seals, and I heard, as it were the noise of thunder, one of the four beasts saying, Come and see.*
>
> ² *And I saw, and behold a white horse: and he that sat on him had a bow; and a crown was given unto him: and he went forth conquering, and to conquer.*

The world is run by politics, banks, and major corporations, not regular, average, everyday people, but by an elite group of men. We rarely question their purpose or intent. I asked myself, do the people we think run the world actually make their own decisions or are they being told what to do by a group of men with even more power? You see, the word "bow" means bending the head or body or knee as a sign of reverence or submission or worship. After submitting to their will, then a crown is given to them meaning a powerful position, and with that power, they go forth doing the will of the fallen, following orders, conquering, and influencing the world. They make you an offer of power and wealth, the same way Lucifer offered to Christ.

> **Luke 4:5-8**
>
> ⁵ *And the devil, taking him up into an high mountain, shewed unto him all the kingdoms of the world in a moment of time.*
>
> ⁶ *And the devil said unto him, All this power will I give thee, and the glory of them: for that is delivered unto me; and to whomsoever I will I give it.*
>
> ⁷ *If thou therefore wilt worship me, all shall be thine.*
>
> ⁸ *And Jesus answered and said unto him, Get thee behind me, Satan: for it is written, Thou shalt worship the Lord thy God, and him only shalt thou serve.*

That is why I believe these powerful rulers who run and control the world never leave anything to chance. I believe we only live with the illusion that we the people control the outcome of major decisions that affect us all. Rulers make us feel like it's our choice, but really, they've already decided who they want to be in power and are waiting until the day they can have absolute power and control of the world. Take our former president, George W. Bush. He was elected into office after a problem with the ballots in Florida, a state that is controlled by his brother, former Governor Jeb Bush. It was because of the ballot recount that Bush was elected president. George W. Bush served two terms and some say he was by far the worst president in the history of the United States of America. Then Barack Obama came along out of nowhere with the promise of change, something America desperately needed. Nobody paid attention to the fact that he was protected like he was already president before being elected. In politics, nothing is left to chance. Everything is controlled, because they have to maintain balance and power. I'm going to tell you about the important people to look at in history, the people I believe to be in control, and what it is they have done.

I don't think anybody truly knows when the doctrine of the Illuminati was formed or when they were truly formed, but when you look at the most powerful people in the world, like the Freemasons, the Skull and Bones, the Rothschild family, and various elite bloodlines around the world, you always find symbolism that was used by King Solomon and the Knights Templar. King Solomon was known in the Bible as a man who was given a gift of wisdom and knowledge from God.

> **1 Kings 3:12**
> *¹² Behold, I have done according to thy words: lo, I have given thee a wise and an understanding heart; so that there was none like thee before thee, neither after thee shall any arise like unto thee.*

God gave Solomon a gift, and with that gift, I believe he understood life, the universe, and the heavens and earth. Which brings me to my next point: if Solomon was blessed, knew God, and still turned his back on him, how was he any different than Lucifer? The Bible says it was because of his lust for women, but he had to have had a deeper understanding of what he was worshipping with the knowledge given to him from God. Solomon knew exactly who and what he was worshiping. Solomon was a king, and he took many women as wives, and one of them was Egyptian, and it is because of his marriage to her that he began to worship Egyptian pagan gods. Then at the end of his life, some believe Solomon turned back to God. Many believe that, because at the end of his life, Solomon wrote about all the mistakes he made in his life, but nobody really knows if he ever found his way back to God. One would be led to believe that is all there was to Solomon. That is, until a text was found telling a more detailed history of King Solomon that the Bible doesn't talk about. The document is called "The Testaments of Solomon." It tells a story of Solomon not only being able to cast out demons, but being able to collect them, conjure them up, and control them using a ring given to him by an angel. It also states that Solomon's Temple was built with the help of demons. Even Christ in the book of Luke referred to Solomon after casting out a demon during an exorcism.

> **Luke 11:31**
> *³¹ The queen of the south shall rise up in the judgment with the men of this generation, and condemn them: for she came from the utmost parts of the earth to hear the wisdom of Solomon; and, behold, a greater than Solomon is here.*

Throughout history we see signs of ancient civilizations claiming that beings from the heavens physically lived here on earth, they were praised as gods, and that they poured vast amounts of knowledge into civilizations. If Solomon could conjure up demons, then he could have gained a vast amount of knowledge and understanding from them, and remember, he was also given knowledge by God. Those two things could have helped him to understand the knowledge that fallen angels taught ancient civilizations and then left behind. If Solomon did have a ring of power, what happened to it? If he did gain knowledge from God himself or any other source, did he ever create any type of hidden writings? Even if he did create writings and they were neither good nor evil, and they were just the key to understanding what was left behind by earlier civilizations that would have still been an important element to look at while trying to figure out how the world got to the point it is at today.

The hexagram and pentagram are symbols King Solomon used and have been linked to supernatural powers since ancient times. They have been said to have been linked to magic, witchcraft, astrology, sorcery, occult organizations, and to some organizations that have been said to be just plain evil. That makes me wonder, when the Knights Templar went to Jerusalem, what did they find in the foundation of Solomon's Temple? We know that the Knights Templar dug through solid rock under the temple for nine years in search of something. I believe they found a cornerstone or a document filled with a vast amount of knowledge. We know from Freemason rituals in building that they bury cornerstones with vast amounts of knowledge and secrets in them. Before finding whatever the Knights found under Solomon's temple, they took an oath to live a life of poverty. They were even known as the "Poor Fellow-Soldiers of Christ and the Temple of Solomon" and also the "Order of the Temple." After finding whatever they found, the Knights left Jerusalem and went back to France.

Have you ever heard the phrase "knowledge is power"? Well, they gained a massive amount of power, and many believed they only answered to the Pope and were granted unlimited power. King Philip IV of France was even in debt to the Knights at the time. The Knights lived above the law and made their own rules, because everyone was either in debt to them or scared of them. King Philip realized how much power and control they gained, and because of their secret initiations and ritual meetings, it created trust issues. The king later ordered them to be arrested and tortured into confession. The Knights confessed to doing satanic acts and initiations. Some were executed and others faced a lifetime of imprisonment. Some believe that a few of the Knights were warned about the arrest. They got away and went on to form the Freemasons. I, however, believe that some of the Knights got away, but the Freemasons were formed long before that time, that King Solomon may have created them, been a part of them, or entrusted them to hide something for him under the temple. If stone masons did hide something for King Solomon, they would have had the same principles Freemasons have today. The Freemasons of today are secretive and believe in protecting ancient knowledge. The man said to be the chief architect of Solomon's Temple was a Grand Master Freemason named Hiram Abiff. He was tortured and killed, because he didn't give up the secret password shared by Master Masons.

It is still unclear what it was the Knights Templar found when in Jerusalem, but I believe whatever it was led to them gaining a massive amount of wealth, power, and control. They became a group of knights who gained even more wealth and power than the King of France, and that is what led them to their deaths. Some of the remaining Templars were believed to have fled to Scotland, and that's where we get the biggest clue to what they found. Some believe that the Sinclair family built or allowed the Templars to stay in Rosslyn Castle, a place where the Knights could study, discover, learn, and teach whatever it was that they found. We see signs that they may have inhabited the castle for almost two hundred years, enough time to let the name of the Knights Templar fade away. After building the castle and learning and growing in knowledge, William Sinclair decided to build a chapel. Rosslyn Chapel is said to have been built to hide artifacts, knowledge, and maybe even treasure collected by the Knights Templar. It may also be the tomb and final resting place of those Templar Knights who escaped from France. If the Templar Knights were religious men of Christ, why is the chapel decorated in not only traditional symbols of the church, but pagan symbols, pentagrams, and Masonic symbols? Aleister Crowley even believed the Knights were fellow devil worshippers. Another question I asked is why the chapel was built to have strategic orientation to astronomical events, like ancient temples and pyramids. It is also a direct replica of part of Solomon's Temple. I believe that by understanding the chapel, we can get closer to understanding what they found. Whatever it was, Solomon built a temple over it trying to hide it. That lets me know how important it was for whatever they found not to fall into the wrong hands.

In the 1500s, a man came along who composed books on how to gain power, wealth, and control and keep it. Niccoló Machiavelli was famous for the book he wrote on politics, control, and power, called *The Prince*. He observed people in politics in courts and composed books on what they needed to do to be more effective in their positions. He spoke on how a person needed to be cruel, ruthless, and a good liar, and must know how to break his word, while still looking like a collected, calm, compassionate human being with good morals. This is a book that a lot of the world's leaders have read, and if they haven't read it, they still follow the rules to power in the book. The book is basically a book of guidelines on how to gain and keep power. It states that rulers have to protect their power at all times, because without their power, they're nothing. It talks about how to have effective leadership in politics, government, corporations, and how to pick staff. He basically wrote the handbook on how to be corrupt but still look as though you're a saint. After publishing a few books, Machiavelli was accused of conspiracy then jailed and tortured. He was later set free by denying his involvement in any conspiracy. Whether he was involved in a conspiracy or not, he was one of the most influential people in perfecting the craft of gaining power, having control, being cruel, and being able to hide a true agenda from the public eye.

When I think about the world's history, a few time periods pop into mind. One time is when ancient civilizations were advanced with no clear explanation as to how they invented certain things, knew any of the things they knew, or built any of the great artifacts or monuments still standing to this day. The one thing we do know is that ancient civilizations claimed that some type of beings came from the heavens and stayed with them, teaching them everything they knew. Then we have a radical church era when man wasn't so advanced. It's almost like after the mysterious disappearances of the ancient civilizations, man became less intelligent. Some even believed that the earth was flat when ancient civilizations knew it was round. Those radical churches were about power and most of the religious leaders claimed to be able to speak directly to God. They used it to control mankind, kill people, go to war, and commit all types of evil in the name of God. Then you have the time of Christ, when he taught man how to live, be good people, love, and live life free. He shed light on how man was supposed to live. That life wasn't about control or the worship of many gods. It was about being free and loving one God (the creator) and loving our neighbors. Then we have an era were man was still living in what most would call the Dark Ages, but a few groups of men began to advance rapidly and understand math, science, and astronomy. People were meeting in secret, coming up with philosophies, better ways to bank, and more ways to gain control. Some people started practicing sorcery and witchcraft. They started to understand and believe in astrology. They started inventing and coming up with different theories like the laws of gravity and the Copernican theory. People started looking at the world with reason and a more rational point of view in life. I believe whatever Solomon buried was the key to understanding the knowledge left behind by pagan gods and even Lucifer himself.

After the knowledge revolution began, the more the church tried to hide things, shoot down ideas, kill and punish people for their scientific, mathematical, or astronomical beliefs and discoveries, and the more they were proven incorrect, the more people believed in gaining knowledge and what the pagan gods left behind.

Soon, there were a lot of people who started thinking with reason and stopped believing in the teachings of the church. More and more, people started to believe, not so much in pagan gods, but in the knowledge they left behind. They started to believe that they, too, could become gods by perfecting themselves. It is the doctrine of Lucifer himself; it's what he promised Eve in the Garden of Eden. A lot of those people were prominent, established men of power spread out all over the world. They convinced people and spread their philosophies and teachings all over the world to grow in numbers, but it wasn't until they got organized and pulled all of those men and resources together with the same belief that they were truly successful in their plans.

In 1776 Adam Weishaupt formed a group of powerful men with the same views as him called the "Order of the Illuminati." That sounds kind of close to the "Order of the Temple." He assembled the group of men set to go forth conquering, controlling, and influencing so that their true plans could be carried out. They would need people to infiltrate different governments and religions to help gain control and to influence decisions that best suited the plans of the elite. The Illuminati wanted to bring knowledge and science into the church and were politically driven. They believed that religious beliefs got in the way of science, knowledge, and research. They dedicated their lives to exploring scientific truth, math, astrology, and astronomy. They planned on overthrowing all religion and all governments. While traveling by horseback carrying a letter explaining the order's plan, an Illuminati courier named Lanze was struck by lightning. That led to the exposure of the Illuminati's plans and the upcoming French Revolution. The Illuminati's beliefs conflicted with the church's beliefs, and after the government discovered their plans, they ordered the arrest and massacre of all Illuminati members in Bavaria, Europe, the birthplace of the Order. The Illuminati had already spread throughout Europe and the Bavarian government couldn't stop the members that had already left to spread their influence in other governments.

Weishaupt and other members were forced into hiding, and the Illuminati vowed that they would stay a secret and in hiding until they were too powerful to be stopped and their goal had been completed. That they would stay hiding in plain sight until the time was right and they could create a new world under them. The New World Order is a world controlled by one government and one religion.

> **Adam Weishaupt**
> *The great strength of our Order lies in its concealmen; let it never appear in any place in its own name, but always covered by another name, and another occupation. None is fitter then Freemasonry, the public is accustomed to it and expects little from it and therefore takes little notice from it. It can only be obtained through secret societies. (www.bilderberg.org/lucis.htm)*

After planning to hide within the Freemasons, the Freemasons organization grew in power and in numbers. Which tells me they succeeded in hiding in the organizations. Some of the most powerful men in the world are and were Freemasons, or people who profited from a member of the Freemason's decisions.

The Freemasons are a fraternity, and fraternity's welcome open worship of any religion, as long as they pay respect to whatever the fraternity stands for and the name of the organization. They believe in following the ranks, and they definitely believe in keeping their word. They're the perfect tools to use to get ahead in a world run by rules, regulations, and money. Secret societies, fraternities, the mafia, the military, and even some of the world's biggest gangs may all be connected to the Illuminati. They would want to make you believe that none of them were connected at all, but why do you think it's so easy to get ahead once you join these groups? Among these groups of people, there are only a few elite members that actually know the real intent and plan of the organization. Not all the people in secret societies and fraternities are bad, because like I said, only a few really know the real intent, but every one of its members still has a purpose. What do they all have in common? They all have rituals and ceremonies to honor ancient pagan gods and goddesses. Whether they are Egyptian, Greek, or any other ancient pagan gods or goddesses, it doesn't matter. They use symbolism used by King Solomon (pentagrams and hexagrams). I believe each of the groups they control are different groups that know nothing about what the other groups are doing, that have different tasks, but are in service to the same goal. Remember, Solomon fell out of God's grace because of pagan worship. Why would it be any different in today's times? Almost everything we do or celebrate has some type of pagan origin, and most of us don't even know it.

After the discovery of the Illuminati, the Bavarian government sent out warnings that the Illuminati had spread. George Washington, a Grand Master Freemason, was elected the first so-called president of the United States, serving two terms from April 30, 1789, until March 4, 1797. After his term in office in 1798, George Washington acknowledged that Illuminati activity had come to America.

> **George Washington**
> *It is not my intention to doubt that the doctrine of the Illuminati and the principles of Jacobinism had not spread in the United States. On the contrary, no one is more satisfied of this fact then I am. (http://www.bibiliotecapleyades.net/ sociopoliticalesp_sociopol_illuminati_31.htm)*

I say so-called first president, because I believe there were presidents before him. He was just the first president who was part of the Illuminati in the United States. I believe that is why there are known Illuminati symbols on the one-dollar bill, like the pyramid with the Eye of Horus. After getting organized and gaining wealth, the Illuminati used secret societies and fraternities to infiltrate different governments, corporations, and religions to ensure their forward progress. They aggressively positioned themselves in powerful positions and created debt systems. They also built great monuments and landmarks with hidden meanings behind them, in which only they would understand, like the Washington Monument, which is an Egyptian obelisk, or the Statue of Liberty, which many would say is a pagan goddess, but clearly shows a lot of resemblance to and wears the crown of the sun god, Lucifer. I even had a chance to check out downtown Washington, DC. It was the most pagan place I have ever seen in my life. After positioning themselves in governments all around the world, the Illuminati created one conspiracy after another to take control and gain wealth. Some believe they were even backed with the Templar treasure. They have set up money systems and ways to get people into debt, used the stock market, created wars, recruited members, blackmailed, controlled the media, used technology and schools to manipulate and brainwash society, poisoned us from the time we were born, and carefully monitored and controlled everything we do.

They created banking systems to keep countries and the people who live in them in debt. After all, the Knights Templar were the first to come up with the loan system. They bought land, used the stock market to gain wealth, and have control over the world's economy. They financially backed, bought shares in, and built up successful businesses. Then they move there businesses and department stores with cheaper prices into every neighborhood. They knock out all the competitors, the small businesses that were built from the ground up that weren't able to compete with their prices. They also own a large amount of the world's gold. The Illuminati secretly control and own almost everything, because their resources are unlimited and they monitor everything carefully. Which means if they don't own the company directly, in some way they still control the outcome of other companies, because you still buy from them.

Barack Obama
If you were successful, somebody along the line gave you some help. There was a great teacher somewhere in your

life. Somebody helped to create this unbelievable American system that we have allowed you to thrive. Somebody invested in roads and bridges. If you've got a business you didn't build that. Somebody else made that happen. (https://en.m.wikipedia.org/wiki/you_didn't_build_that)

They pretend like they are not all connected, when really they all have the same ruler and work towards the same goal. It is just carefully hidden by using different names and different corporations. Now I want you to remember this Bible scripture and think about everything I am saying very carefully.

Proverbs 22:7
⁷ The rich rule over the poor, and the borrower is a slave to the lender.

They figured out a way for countries to be in a continuous and growing debt to them. It is called a central banking system and it gives a private company control over how much money is printed, how much money is loaned to a country, and how much interest should be on the loan given. That means that the private company controls every aspect of a nation's money. That means they have complete control of a country, and since they have the country in a never ending debt, they would invest money into the stock market, buy shares in corporations, buy land, buy gold, and basically control the nation's economy and its decisions.

Mayer Amschel Rothschild
Let me issue and control a nation's money and I care not who writes the laws. (http://www.iamthewitness.com/darylbradfordsmith_rothschild.htm)

I see now why Mayer Rothschild made that statement. It is because if you control a nation's money and they're in debt to you, like France was in debt to the Templars, you're granted unlimited power and become above the law. President Woodrow Wilson signed the bill giving the Illuminati power over America's money when most of Congress was away on Christmas vacation. The bill made the Federal Reserve Bank our central banking system, and after passing the bill, he replied by saying this:

> **Woodrow Wilson**
> I am a most unhappy man. I have unwittingly ruined my country. A great industrial nation is controlled by its system of credit. Our system of credit is concentrated. The growth of the nation, therefore, and all our activities are in the hands of a few men. We have come to be one of the worst ruled, one of the most completely controlled and dominated governments in the civilized world no longer a government by free opinion, no longer a government by conviction and the vote of a majority, but a government by the opinion and duress of a small group of dominant men. (http://en.m.wikiquote.org/wiki/talk:woodrow_wilson)

It's not just America, though; almost every country in the world is controlled by a system of credit. All central banking systems are run and controlled by the Illuminati. So if your country borrows money from another country, it's still getting its money from a banking system. All of the elite's money is protected and kept private by big banks and kept in vaults underground. Well, at least the gold is kept underground. They have so many ways of hiding their wealth, you will never truly know how much they are worth. Our countries are in so much debt now who's even counting? In this world gold, silver, land, human labor, animals, diamonds, and oil are all worth something. Credit is just a way to get people in debt with money that never even existed. The pieces of paper that we call money are worth nothing. It is nothing but an "I owe you" note to the Federal Reserve Bank, which is why on money it says "Federal Reserve Note." Our countries are slaves to central banking systems, and we are slaves to our countries and their laws. The Federal Reserve Bank even owns your name. It's how they borrow from other countries. It's not you, but your parents who sign your rights away at the time of your birth.

When you are born, the government takes out a loan from the Federal Reserve Bank, and they put it into your "straw man name." A straw man name, a fiction or trademark, is a name that is put in all capital letters or has your last name first on a document. The only time a person's name means that he is a living human being is when his name appears the right way on a document. Here's an example of the correct way to spell a living human being's name: John Doe. In a country where your name is spelled with all capital letters or first name last, you fall into the jurisdiction of their laws and regulations. It's almost like when you're born they make your name a corporation; they borrow money for it and it grows in interest, but you don't have access to the company money, and you have to follow the company's rules. That is why your name is in all capital letters on all of your personal identification. As long as we acknowledge that fiction name they created, they can take away every God-given right we have. In return for the loan, the government promises that you will work in your lifetime, be a slave, borrow, and take out loans for everything. The government still has to pay back the loan, and the only way to pay the interest is to borrow more money or offer something of value to them. It is a never ending debt system that just keeps growing with time. It has grown so much that they have unlimited access to our nation's resources. The banking system is controlled by the Illuminati. They are the lenders, and no matter how we look at it, we are the borrowers. They want everyone to be in debt to them, which is why the cost of living is always going up. It is the debt that establishes their control over the world. Soon it won't be your debt that gives them control; it will be your need to live and your fear that gives them power. The economy and the stock market play a major role in them successfully completing their plan for world domination.

Economy: *a careful, thrifty management of resources such* *as money, materials, and labor (http://www.thefreedictionary.com/economy)*

The stock market shows how well the economy is doing. The Illuminati have not only used the stock market to gain wealth, but now they completely control and manipulate it, always to their advantage. The stock market shows how much people buy, sell, and trade and allows people to be able to invest in corporate companies. The fluctuation in the stock market determines what companies survive and/or make a profit or how many people will be unemployed or have a job the morning after a drastic change in numbers. The economy and the stock market showed me that the power of our country's survival is in their hands. That one day you can be living your life, and the next minute you can be worried about how you're going to feed your family, because you are completely dependent on them and their system. They have used top companies as fronts to hide their money or to further establish their control of the stock market and the world's economy. Most, if not all, of the world's leaders in finances are part of the plan. They control the outcome of every country's fate and the survival of the people in them. That is unless we change and take away the power they have over us by learning to survive on our own. Anytime you are dependent on a system for survival you are a slave to it and whoever owns that system.

> **David Rockefeller**
> *Some even believe we are part of a secret cabal working against the best interests of the united states, characterizing my family and me as 'internationalists' and of conspiring with others around the world to build a integrated global political and economic structure—one world, if you will. If that's the charge, I stand guilty, and I am proud of it. (https://www.metabunk.org/anyone-cape-to-debunk-these-two-rockefeller-quotes.t431/)*

After setting up central banking systems, the Illuminati created wars to make countries further in debt. They used wars and banks to manipulate countries' economies into poverty. Countries would have no choice but to turn to a central banking system for help if they wanted to have a chance at winning the war the Illuminati created. The countries at war would have to take out major loans from the central banking system. Any way you look at it, the central banking system profits from a war, because all that money is insured by the government, so whoever wins has to pick up the bill of the loser. Not to mention that the Illuminati own the private military companies that countries give all the contracts to so that when the smoke clears, the Illuminati profit a great deal from war. In any war, they emerge the victors. They use wars to create hatred among us, gain wealth, and gain control, and they to push hate to fuel wars and guide society into a direction that most benefits the Illuminati. They concentrate on our differences and promote them to cause hate. Since the French Revolution, there hasn't been a war that wasn't orchestrated and carefully planned by them.

To grow, progress, and keep the plan alive, they would have had to have control over what we learn in school to make us smarter, more open-minded, controlled, and obedient. They force us to believe in certain principles and the version of history they want us to see. They wait and collectively pick students who excel in the curriculum they have created. They recruit only the most intelligent students out of Ivy League schools and mold them to take on powerful positions. After all, the more intelligent you are, the more rational you are and the more you think with reason. They make you pledge your loyalty to them. They make you give them the control, and when you do, they reward you generously.

One of the most powerful known fraternities, or should I say secret societies, that recruits and molds its members into powerful positions is the Skull and Bones. Some of the most powerful men in this world have come from this organization, including the members of Bush family. The elite also use entertainers who people believe in and that have a manipulative influence on the public and who are completely dedicated to the elite's purpose. After being recruited, they have to make a sacrifice to show their total submission to the will of the order. This could be a blood sacrifice (the death of a loved one, like a family member or someone very close to them). Committing homosexual acts with someone in the Order who has more power (which could be used to blackmail the newly recruited). Those are the two most common rituals/initiation acts I have heard about, but I am sure there are other ways they bow before the Order.

See, knowingly submitting to the will of the Order does not mean you are in the Illuminati; it means you work for them, you're just part of the plan. It means that you to believe in Lucifer's philosophy and you love power and wealth and to be worshipped like a God. It is a drug that keeps you addicted; you just keep wanting more. After submitting to the will of the Order, people's lives are set, so they become rich and powerful. Then they place those people in powerful positions or boost their already promising careers to assist in carrying out their plan for world domination. It's almost like a game of chess and they have been strategically setting up their pieces. Sorry to say, it's a game that we have been losing for a very long time. They are the leaders of companies, majority stock holders, owners of lucrative businesses, politicians, legislative branches, your favorite entertainers, and even religious leaders. They are everywhere and could be anyone, including someone you've known your whole life. People would sell their souls just to get wealthy, but as it says in the book of Matthew:

> **Matthew 16:26**
> [26] *For what is a man profited, if he shall gain the whole world, and lose his own soul? or what shall a man give in exchange for his soul?*

This world is controlled by money and they control what we call money. They can make all of your financial problems disappear. They can make your dreams come true. They can make you a celebrity and worshipped by many, but is it worth your soul? Is a piece of paper worth nothing an even trade for your soul? Some people choose that way because their minds are controlled. They believe that money will somehow solve all of their problems. That people will love and accept them for having it. I guess I can't blame them, because I used to think money could solve all my problems before I realized the deception. They have used everything around us to brainwash us so that we may never figure out the meaning of life, their plan, and that we are controlled and influenced by them. The only difference between the paper we call money and fake money used in a board game is the belief that one is of higher value then the other. If you don't believe you are influenced or controlled, think about socialism and when it came into existence and what it really means.

Satan was the most beautiful angel, and he was created perfect. Many believe because of that he was worshipped up in heaven and wanted more power. Satan was in charge of the entertainment in heaven. He was the angel of music. What is the number one requirement to being in entertainment? You must be attractive to the public eye to capture the interest of your audience. Once you have gained the interest of your audience, you deliver a message to them, whether it is through music, words, hidden messages, television programs, the internet, or through any other form of communication; especially when watching TV. Why do you think they call a television show a program? They put attractive people on TV to spark your interest, and then they feed you messages to program your mind. Entertainment tells the world what is in and what is out. It tells you what's accepted and what's not accepted in society. It tells you how to act and you start to see a trend were people start to dress like, talk like, and even act like their favorite entertainers. They can feed you a few little messages to get you to buy something, and then you buy something worth five dollars for hundreds, maybe even thousands of dollars, because of a name brand. They can get the majority of society to do just about anything with all the mind-altering technologies of today. If you're thinking that watching television doesn't have an influence on people, think about this. If it doesn't have any effect on people, then why would people pay almost four million dollars for a Super Bowl commercial for ten seconds if it wasn't going to make people go out and buy their product?

They're hiding amongst us in plain sight, manipulating and brainwashing our minds and influencing our choices. They control everything we hear and see. It's propaganda in its highest form. We think we are making our own choices in life when really it's what they programmed our minds to do, want, and believe. Through the use of technology, they secretly pushed the world into the brainwashed civilization we see today. When you know too much, start to speak out against them, are planning to expose them, speak of freedom, or don't obey their orders and you are a public figure, you become a threat to them. I guess you could see how John Lennon, Jimmy Hendricks, John Todd, Martin Luther King, Jr., Bob Marley, John F. Kennedy, Michael Jackson, Princess Diana, Malcolm X, Tupac Shakur, and William Cooper could have been a threat to them. All of these influential great people who stood up for what they believed in were all assassinated, are missing, or suffered tragic, unexpected death. Coincidence? I think not. Christ was killed because by telling the truth about life and showing mankind the right way to live, he became a threat to the controlled way of living. He became a danger to a society built on deception, illusions, and lies. So every time anyone even has a fragment of the truth and speaks out about the right thing to do, they become hated by those that are caught in the deception, the wicked. Sure, some people will love you, but ultimately, the world will hate you, because they love living in this dream world of lies.

John 15:18

[15] *If the world hates you, ye know that it hated me before it hated you.*

The truth is, most people would rather hear a lie than the truth. Soon after telling the truth, you become a target to those who feel threatened or who think they're doing the right thing. It saddens me when I see lost people who refuse to see the truth, because they are blinded by the ways of the world.

They also have used other methods in affecting our minds, except this method makes us more submissive and controlled, kills us, and makes us crazy. They have poisoned us using water, medicine, and food, and they even release it into the air. They are putting mind-altering chemicals in our water. In 1954 a Nazi German chemist wrote a letter to the Lee Foundation for Nutritional Research.

> **Charles Perkins**
> *Repeated doses of infinitesimal amounts of fluoride will in time reduce an individual's power to resist domination, by slowly poisoning and narcotizing a certain area of the brain, thus making him submissive to the will of those who wish to govern him. (http:www.rense.com/general79/hd3.htm)*

Not only do they use water to make you more submissive and subjugated, but they make people sterile through medicine. They give people medicines to cure one thing and it makes them even sicker in a whole other way. Sometimes they even tell people it will happen: have you ever seen the commercials on TV telling you to try a drug and it has a long list of other symptoms and side effects? They put poisons on the food they grow, rinse it off, and then feed it to us. I remember the stories my grandfather told me on how people used to stick together and have their own gardens. It's sad to say that it seems like in today's times everybody is out for themselves. He explained to me that when he was growing up, everything was organic and, all they used to grow their gardens was the soil. Recently, they have tried to pass laws preventing people from growing their own gardens in the comfort of their own homes. I guess they want to make sure we're eating the poison they produce.

AN ORGANIZED PLAN

I ask myself every day why they would want to stop us from having a garden when part of the world is experiencing a drought of rain and water and not producing enough crops. You would think they would encourage everyone to have one to help feed others. In the last few months, I have been hearing stories about farmers facing jail time for trying to help the poor. Farmer's being shut down because of the lack of workers due to immigration laws. The government wants to regulate and control every piece of farmland. They inject animals with steroids, mercury, and different poisons, and then they expect us to cook and eat the poisons they produce without saying anything about it. Have you ever seen that chicken leg in the grocery store that looked almost as big as a human leg and thought to yourself that there was no way that it could have come from a chicken? If you want to go hunting or raise animals to kill and eat for yourself, there are laws preventing it. I don't even think you can have chickens in the city anymore. You can only hunt certain animals at specific times of year and you have to register and have a license to do so. There is a regulation on people being able to hunt and provide for their families. They tell us there's a certain way you have to kill animals because of animal cruelty or because of public safety. Then I saw the way they slaughter animals in the slaughterhouse; it's one of the cruelest things I have ever seen. We live in a world where they want everything to be completely dependent on them. We don't do anything for ourselves anymore, and the people that knew how to take care of everything on their own are old or dead; a new generation is here. Sorry to say we will be left helpless to what is coming, and nobody can hide from it. One of the most recent things I found out they were doing is spilling chemicals into the air. Every day you walk outside you have been breathing it in and it is even being absorbed through your skin. They are called Chemtrails, but I will get to those a little later in the book, because I have yet to tell you the main purpose of those mysterious lines in the sky.

It seems as though we are in prison, because you can't just get up and do what you want, when you want every day, because they tell you it's uncivilized, unlawful, or unholy. There's always somebody watching and monitoring everything we do. Keeping us in order and telling us what we can and can't do. You always have somewhere you have to be and someone controlling when you have to be there. You always have rules and laws to follow and someone to make sure that you follow them. The government can listen to, watch, or locate you wherever you are in the world using technology, especially since 9/11 happened and the USA PATRIOT Act was passed. That gives the government unlimited access to take away your privacy and monitor everything you do. Make no mistake, there is someone monitoring and watching everything you do. They could even be watching you read this book right now.

I believe the elite control all of the government agencies, but the organization doing the monitoring is the Central Intelligence Agency. The CIA was created by secret societies and is still controlled and run by them today. The newest group they formed goes by the name Fusion, which takes everything you say, do, or believe and fuses all your information together and decides whether you are a threat to those in power or not. Fusion is funded by the government and bankers, but not controlled or regulated by the government, which allows them to do just about whatever they want. They are now invading all of your privacy, taking whatever information they want. I know what you're thinking; you haven't done anything wrong, so you're not worried. Well, you should be, because there have already been cases of children as well as adults being snatched out of homes and imprisoned, and nobody can figure out why or what crime they have committed.

Just to give you a few examples about what I mean when I say you're not free to do as you please and you're being watched. They have a machine that monitors everything you do electronically, listens to and records your phone conversations. Even if your phone is turned off, they can still listen to everything around you if the battery is still in your phone. If you say one of the keywords the system is programmed to listen for, that conversation is reported or monitored. Sometimes they even turn on your camera phone to see who that person is who is talking. Social networks record everything you do and say. Then sell it to different corporations and the government. They put tracking device on everything that's mobile or connected to a network. I've even heard rumors of there being chips in our new state identification cards and driver's licenses. There are cameras everywhere watching our every move. If you know someone's address, type it in your computer. The map on the internet will show you the exact house through a satellite stream. Every new car and phone has a GPS tracking signal in it, and they can track down any person within a few feet; all they need is the telephone number you use. Why do you think the government is giving so many free phones away? They are going out of their way making commercials and mailing out letters begging people to get a free phone. They even set up tents in communities and give them out for free. Everything we have come to love that makes our lives feel easier or supposedly safer will be the same things they use against us in the end. When everything starts to come under their rule, how do you think they will find you? They already know where you are, who you are, and if you could be a possible threat to them.

While everything in the world is controlled and monitored, we can still choose to be free. Being free is a state of mind, and when you find peace, it's a lifestyle. The truth is, most people simply don't want to be free, because they're comfortable with who they are and the life they live. We will never have complete freewill to make a choice in our lives unless we change as a whole and take back the rights that every living human being on earth is given at birth by God. Unless we choose to rely on ourselves and God for everything and not on the power of another, we will never be free, because being free is not about control; it's a choice. Most people feel like they're making their own choices in life, but if they regulate the options people have, then people choose one of the options given. Did people really make their own choice? I believe most people are really just influenced, forced into doing something, or left with only the options given to them and choose from them. They don't even know they're being controlled and they really don't care enough to pay attention.

As long as we still need them, we will never be free. We've been taught since birth that this is how we are supposed to live our lives, and because it's easier or convenient, we accept it. Your mind is the product, and they know all your characteristics and have been programming you to be who you are since birth. It's easy to influence, control, or change a person's mind if you control everything around them his whole life. They've done it over time and created distractions so it would be hard to notice that we are doing and thinking exactly what they want us to. Especially since they have created and control the educational systems established around the world. There is no doubt in my mind that these Luciferians have spread, grown, and advanced. They now completely run and control the world. Which makes me ask the question, what or who are they waiting for? They've been so secretive that most people don't believe they exist. Similar to how a lot of people don't even believe that the devil exists. The greatest trick the devil ever pulled was making people think he didn't exist. Sounds to me like the Illuminati borrowed the devil's greatest trick. Just because you don't think something exists, doesn't mean that you're safe from it. You see, the Latin word *illuminatus* means "enlightened" and that's where the Illuminati gets their name from. They are very enlightened about the real history of this earth, ancient knowledge, and the false light-bearer's (Lucifer's) plan to rule the world, and they will stop at nothing to complete their task. They infiltrate and control everything nowadays; they have even influenced and deceived most of the churches of today.

CHAPTER 7

TESTIMONY OF THE TRUE CHURCH

When I lost my job after George W. Bush was in office, with no jobs hiring, I didn't have a choice but to get on unemployment. I could barely pay my bills, and one of my bills was traffic tickets. I ended up spending two weeks in jail for traffic tickets that I didn't want to pay and really couldn't pay. When I got there, I noticed something about almost every person locked up with me. They all came to jail searching for a better understanding of God, not only to ask for forgiveness, but an understanding on what to do in a world designed for them to fail, struggle, stress, and be left in a state of depression. How can we make it in a world designed for us to rely on a group of people working for someone with one purpose, to gain our soul?

A day after I got locked up, a man who was hooked on smoking crack, among other drugs, got put in the same cell as me. There were eight people assigned to each cell, and this man came in and started preaching to other cellmates. Even though he was a drug addict, to my surprise, some of the other cellmates sat and listened to what he had to say. I mean, usually when you're hooked on drugs as strong as that, people don't treat you like you're human.

The other half of the cell just wanted the crack smoking junky to shut up. Still, I just sat back and watched as the people sat around listening. A crack smoker talking about religion was the funniest thing in the world, just because he used it to get stuff from other inmates. I can still hear his voice saying, "God told me that you was gonna bless me with a pack of noodles or some of them chips." I can also still hear some of the other inmates telling him, "God told me to tell you to go sit your ass down." Seeing those men sit around him as he spoke made me think to myself, why didn't any of the people in my cell have any direction as to what God wanted from them, and why couldn't they find it from church on the outside? I guess when you are in jail you don't have all the distraction the world puts in front of you. I guess without all the distractions, you have a lot of time to breathe deeply. I still asked myself a lot of questions, trying to discover why that was; I mean, were they too busy on the outside of jail to give God at least one day of their time? Did they believe in what they were learning in church, or was it too hard to become that good person they really wanted to be in the world we live in? I wanted to answer the questions, but I couldn't. I couldn't answer them, because at the time, I didn't really know. Here I was trying to figure out why they didn't go to church and I hadn't been in over a year.

So when I got out of jail, I started going to different churches, trying to get a grasp on the things that they were teaching. I mean, I had been to church so many times before, but did I really pay attention to what was going on and being taught? After that night in the hood when we figured out what we thought and believed was the meaning of life, church seemed different and something changed in me for forever. I wanted to know the truth about religion and what really happened in history. I started to look at the preachers and priests, talk to Jehovah's Witnesses walking the streets, go to Muslim meetings, and look at other religious leaders in a whole new light. All it did was make me realize how much I hate religion but how much I love God. Every time I went to church, I noticed something different about them all. I would always find things that I liked, but now I was finding things that I thought were terribly wrong. I mean, no church is perfect, I get that, but the things I saw in some of the churches these days broke my heart. I figured out quickly that it wasn't that the people who didn't go to church were evil, but it was the good in them that caused them to see evil in some of these churches. I noticed how most of the religious leaders from church talked about how they were picked by God. How they were prophets, angels, or apostles of the church and could see what God has planned for the people in church. I thought to myself, what really makes them men of God, because they read the Bible a couple dozen times and still don't get the meaning. Is it because they can quote Bible scriptures really well and are great speakers? Then I realized that the church is full of politics and that the Illuminati's influence had spread into the church. A church is not a place where people politic with members and one after another try to impress the person of position above them to climb the ranks.

Churches nowadays use the pyramid effect and that's what makes them easy to control and influence. The pyramid effect is what everything is run by in the world today and it's also how the Illuminati control everything. One person looks over two people. Two people look over four people and so on. Who is at the top of this pyramid is the question. Who decides who becomes a bishop? Then he controls a few churches and then he decides who the preachers will be to direct the flock. Then he decides which obedient members will help to direct the flock. All you have to do is be the person who controls the person in charge and have an influence in the history behind Biblical events, and you have control and influence of the people. The person in charge teaches everyone under him on the pyramid whatever he will have them believe. Then I thought a messenger from God should not be sitting on a throne at church as if he is above everyone else. People shouldn't have to have a license to preach the good news to the world. That license is only to make sure that you believe and have learned the same thing as everyone else. I thought about everything that has been going on in the world and I also thought about the future, and if, in the end, the world is going to switch to one religion. I couldn't believe everything that I was told and taught, because in order to make that transition to one religion in the last days, you would have to have an influence in all religions. It also says that in the end they will imprison and kill people for their names' sake. Well, nobody really hates any of the religious leaders. I know, because they are no threat to evil, at least not yet. When they turn on the people of God, they will think they are doing the right thing in the end, just like the people who had Christ crucified thought they were doing the right thing.

I pray and search for answers myself on what is the truth. I believe the word of God can come from anywhere, but the true message comes from your heart. That it is your heart that the Holy Spirit, Christ, and God speak to, because the true church is inside of you. A person cannot put a license on speaking from the heart and the words spoken cannot be governed by the mind. That's why in Revelations I believe when John was writing letters to actual churches, he was writing to us to warn us about the churches in the present day. I believe he left us a warning of the seven kinds of people and churches we would see in the end of days. So we would not be deceived by their teachings and follow them.

Ephesus
Revelation 2:1–7

¹ Unto the angel of the church of Ephesus write; These things saith he that holdeth the seven stars in his hand, who walketh in the midst of the seven candlesticks:

² I know thy works, and thy labour, and thy patience, and how thou canst not bear them which are evil: and thou hast tried them which say they are apostles, and are not, and hast found them liars:

> *³ And hast borne, and hast patience, and for my name's sake hast laboured, and hast not fainted.*
>
> *⁴ Nevertheless I have somewhat against thee, because thou hast left thy first love.*
>
> *⁵ Remember therefore from whence thou art fallen, and repent, and do the first works; or else I will come unto thee quickly, and I will remove thy candlestick out of his place, except thou repent.*
>
> *⁶ But this thou hast, that thou hatest the deeds of the Nicolaitanes, which I also hate.*
>
> *⁷ He that hath an ear, let him hear what the Spirit saith unto the churches; To him that overcometh will I give to eat of the tree of life, which is in the midst of the paradise of God.*

God knows how you don't like evil and stand against it. How you have found those who say they are of God to be liars. How you have labored in his name teaching the world the truth. Even though you see these people do evil, you are against these people, you still must find away to love them. God's first work is to love even those who are evil. Your first love is God and God is love.

Smyrna
Revelation 2:8–11

> *⁸ And unto the angel of the Smyrna write; These things saith the first and the last, which was dead, and is alive;*
>
> *⁹ I know thy works, and tribulation, and poverty, (but thou art rich) and I know the blasphemy of them which say they are Jews, and are not, but are the synagogue of Satan.*
>
> *¹⁰ Fear none of those things which thou shalt suffer: behold, the devil shall cast some of you into prison, that ye may be tried; and ye shall have tribulation ten days: be thou faithful unto death, and I will give thee a crown of life.*
>
> *¹¹ He that hath an ear, let him hear what the Spirit saith unto the churches; He that overcometh shall not be hurt of the second death.*

Christ says he knows how hard life is and what you are going through. He knows how those that say they are Jews but are not control the world. He says to fear none of the things that will happen and be faithful to him even if it leads to your death.

Pergamos
Revelation 2:12-17

¹² And to the angel of the church in Pergamos write; These things saith he which hath the sword with two edges;

¹³ I know thy works and where thou dwellest, even where Satan's seat is: and thou holdest fast my name, and hast not denied my faith, even in those days wherein Antipas was my faith martyr, who was slain amoung you where Satan dwelleth

¹⁴ But I have few against thee, because thou hast there them that hold the doctrine of Balaam, who taught Balac to cast a stumblingblock before the children of Israel, to eat things sacrificed unto idols, and to commit fornication.

¹⁵ So hast thou also them that hold the doctrine of the Nicolaitans, which thing I hate.

¹⁶ Repent; or else I will come unto thee quickly, and I will fight against them with the sword of my mouth

¹⁷ He that hath an ear, let him hear what the Spirit saith unto the churches; To him that overcometh will I give to eat of the hidden manna, and will give him a white stone, and in the stone a new name written, which no man knoweth saving he that receiveth it.

Christ says that he knows where Satan's seat is and those that eat the things sacrificed to the idols and commit fornication (Illuminati). Hold on to your faith and his name, because many will be killed and become Martyrs for his name's sake. God says that he hates those people's actions (Illuminati) and if they do not repent he will come into us quickly and fight them with the word of God.

Thyatira
Revelations 2:18–29

¹⁸ And unto the angel of the church in Thyatira write; These things saith the son of God, who hath his eyes like unto a flame of fire, and his feet are like fine brass;

¹⁹ I know thy works, and charity, and service, and faith, and thy patience, and thy works; and the last to be more then the first.

²⁰ Notwithstanding I have a few things against thee, because thou sufferest that woman Jezebel, which calleth herself a prophetess, to teach and seduce my servants to commit fornication, and eat things sacrificed unto idols.

²¹ And I gave her space to repent of her fornication; and she repented not.

²² Behold, I will cast her into a bed, and them that commit adultery with her into great tribulation, except they repent of their good deeds.

²³ And I will kill her children with death; and all churches shall know that I am he which searcheth the reins and hearts: and I will give unto every one of you according to your works.

²⁴ But unto you I say, and unto the rest in Thyatira, as many as have not this doctrine, and which have known the depths of Satan, as they speak; I will put upon you none other burden.

²⁵ But that which ye have already hold fast till I come.

²⁶ And he that overcometh, and keepeth my works unto the end, to him I will give the power over the nations:

²⁷ And he shall rule them with a rod of iron; as the vessels of potter shall they be broken to shivers: even as I received of my Father.

²⁸ And I will give him the morning star.

²⁹ He that hath an ear, let him hear what the Spirit saith unto the churches.

Christ says that he knows that the false prophets seem good and they do good deeds, but do not follow them. They will seduce you into doing wrong and following the wrong teachings. We cannot hide from Christ he knows what's in our mind and heart. He will give unto everyone according to what they do. Through all those false teachings do not listen and hold firmly until Christ returns.

Sardis
Revelations 3:1-6
¹ And unto the angel of the church in Sardis write; These things saith he that hath the seven Spirits of God, and the seven stars; I know thy works, that thou hast a name that thou livest, and art dead.

² Be watchful, and strengthen the things which remain, that are ready to die: for I have not found thy works perfect before God.

³ Remember therefore how thou hast received and heard, and hold fast, and repent. If therefore thou shalt not watch, I will come on thee as a thief, and thou shalt not know what hour I will come upon thee.

⁴ Thou hast a few names even in Sardis which have not defiled their garments; and they shall walk with me in white: for they are worthy.

⁵ He that overcometh, the same shall be clothed in white raiment; and I will not blot out his name out of the book of life, but I confess his name before my Father, and before his angels.

⁶ He that hath and ear, let him hear what the Spirit saith unto the churches.

Recognize what is going on in the world, why you act the way you do, and remember the things you have seen and heard about Christ. We should be watchful of the things that are happening with the world, even in church, and hold on to the teachings of Christ. Believe in the basics of faith and truth about Christ. People will try to corrupt your mind by bringing new teachings of Christ into the church. Sometimes even a man of the church's interpretation of what the Bible is saying can be wrong. You have to read it for yourself and pray to the Father for understanding. If you are not watchful and you don't pay attention to the warnings of the seven seals or the warnings Christ gives us about life and the churches, God will come upon you like a thief in the night, and it will be too late to change then, because no man knows the date of his return.

Philadelphia
Revelation 3:7–13

⁷ And to the angel of the church in Philadephia write; These things saith he that is holy, he that is true, he that have the key of David, he that openeth, and no man shutteth; and shutteth, and no man openeth;

⁸ I know thy works: behold, I have set before thee an open door, and no man can shut it: for thou hast a little strength, and hast kept my word, and hast not denied my name.

⁹ Behold, I will make them of the synagogue of Satan, which say they are Jews, and are not, but do lie; behold, I will make them to come and worship before thy feet, and to know that I have loved thee.

¹⁰ Because thou hast kept the word of my patience, I also will keep thee from the hour of temptation, which shall come upon all the world, to try them that dwell upon earth.

¹¹ Behold, I come quickly: hold that fast which thou hast, that no man take thy crown.

¹² Him that overcometh will I make a pillar in the temple of my God, and shall go no more out: and I will write upon him the name of my God, and the name of the city of my God, which is new Jerusalem, which cometh down out of heaven from my God: and I will write upon him my new name.

¹³ He that hath an ear, let him hear what the Spirit saith unto the churches.

The Lord has given people in this day and time jobs to do and has opened doors for them, and no man can stop the will of God. One of God's messengers has kept the word of God and completed the job that he entrusted to him. He kept the faith and patience to God's plan for his children. God will send that person to New Jerusalem to the synagogue of Satan and he will worship at God's feet and Satan will know that God loved him. Which means Satan will recognize the truth and realize God loved that person because he has heard the truth.

Laodiceans
Revelations 3:14–22

14 And to the angel of the church of the Laodiceans write; These things saith the Amen, the faith and true witness, the beginning of the creation of God;

15 I know thy works, that thou art neither cold nor hot: I would thou wert cold or hot.

16 So then because thou art lukewarm, and neither cold nor hot, I will spue thee out of my mouth.

17 Because thou sayest, I am rich, and increased with goods, and have need of nothing; and knowest not that thou are wretched, and miserable, and poor, and blind, and naked:

18 I counsel thee to buy of me gold tried in the fire, that thou mayest be rich; and white raiment, that thou mayest be clothed, and that shame of thy nakedness do not appear; and anointed thine eyes with eyesalve, that thou mayest see.

19 As many as I love, I rebuke and chasten: be zealous therefore, and repent.

20 Behold, I stand at the door, and knock: if any man hear my voice, and open the door, I will come in to him, and will sup with him, and he with me.

21 To him that overcometh will I grant to sit with me in my throne, even as I also overcame, and am set down with my Father in his throne.

> *²² He that hath an ear, let him hear what the Spirit saith unto the churches.*

Nobody should follow, praise, or worship Christ halfway. Offer and devote your life to Christ; the spirit of the Lord should burn within you. Nowadays, most people are not all the way in Christ; they are in the middle, because they don't want to give their life completely over. They let money and material things keep them from being completely in Christ. Those that believe they are rich because they have increased goods, materials, and want for nothing are wretched, miserable, poor, blind, and naked, because we have nothing without a relationship with Christ, only then can someone be considered rich. We should invest our lives in Christ, a gold that has been tried in the fires of hell and died for our sins, but lives again. God punishes us sometimes to bring us closer to him and we should repent and develop a better relationship with God. When you accept Christ in your life, you will realize that you do not need much to be happy.

That is what the seven churches meant to me, in order. After getting an understanding on the seven churches, I started to look at the churches of today with a better understanding of what is of God and what is not. I believe God told John to write Revelations because he knew over time the Bible would be changed, that Satan's followers would have an influence on the church, that people would be blinded by the ways of the world and once again in slavery.

My view on religion and what God wants from us is different from the point of view I have been taught all my life. I believe that throughout history, all of the Bibles have been changed, some a little and others a lot. If they haven't been changed, then I believe they may be missing parts or have lost meaning in some words through translation. If you believe that not to be true, then why would there be so many versions of the Bible, why isn't there just one? Some people believe that King James changed the Bible to make it more like his kingdom. Many others believe that the

Roman pagan emperor Constantine switched over to Christianity and commissioned the Bible to be collected and edited, and decided which parts to rewrite, keep out, and put in. The biggest question is whether he truly was a Christian, because I believe he only pretended to switch to Christianity. My suspicion about Emperor Constantine comes from looking at some of the artifacts he left behind. Also from the fact that some of the Roman Christian churches had sun god temples built right under them. Constantine may have also changed pagan holidays to Christian holidays. He may also be the reason people choose to worship and go to church on Sunday (SUN-day). He may have also changed Christ's and his mother's names to Jesus and Mary. The alphabet in which they used at the time of Christ had no J in it, so where does the name Jesus come from? His real name is "Yahushua," but somehow, it turned into Jesus.

Another thing about the Bible is that most people believe that there were only four Gospels, by Luke, Matthew, Mark, and John, when really there were over thirty Gospels written. Some in these names and some by other authors, like the Gospel of Thomas. Some scholars even claim those Gospels to be of better quality and more in depth and extensive than those found in modern Bibles today. The First Council of Nicaea was a council of Christian bishops and Constantine himself that decided which books of the Bible to keep. The Emperor Constantine was a pagan worshipper who believed in ruling with absolute power, bringing religion and government together, and looking at the artifacts he left behind, that he himself was a living god. His kingdom was falling apart, and the only way he could bring peace to Rome was to switch over to Christianity. I know what you're thinking, this can't be true, the Bible is canonized. Well, even the man who formed the Illuminati, Adam Weishaupt, was a professor of the canon law.

The Bibles have also been translated many times into different languages, and when you translate something into different languages, it loses meaning, because one word could mean so much more in a different language. The Bibles we read today couldn't have been changed much, because many people had already read parts of the Bible before Constantine decided to put them together. The Bible has been rewritten and translated over and over again through the years, and that draws just a little suspicion, even after Constantine. I also believe there may be parts missing to keep us from discovering the truth. Most people in the church don't believe the Bible has been changed at all or could possibly be missing any parts. Every man or woman who owns a Bible, no matter which version or what kind it is, believes what they are reading is perfect. They don't acknowledge the fact that people have found other writings through the years that may have also been inspired by the teachings of Christ or God.

I believe that the King James Version of the Bible is as close to the original Bible as it gets and that it can be perfect if you know how to read it, but that is my belief. That is where I found my truth and it is also where I find my strength in these last days. When I read it, I think of being free and what Christ was really trying to teach with his actions and lifestyle. I think of pure, unconditional love and what the meaning was behind what I read. I think of the fact that God doesn't make mistakes and of the story of Adam and Eve. Even though the book of Genesis speaks of fallen angels physically living with mankind, I found that most churches don't recognize the fact that fallen angels physically lived here on earth with specific civilizations or that a lot of ancient civilizations recorded the fact that those winged beings were actually here on earth, guiding, influencing, and teaching their societies. It is my belief that if we understood what fallen angels tried to teach and the direction they influenced society to go since ancient times, we would understand that the evil, sinful world we live in has been planned by them all along. That what God wanted from us was simple. We would also truly understand what Christ was trying to teach us. How can we understand what has brought us to the end without truly understanding what happened in the beginning.

How can we lead if we are blind? If someone blind leads someone blind, then they will both fall in a pit. Christ didn't tell us everything, because he knew the world wasn't ready to handle the truth. The truth is something we had to discover on our own. He did give us basic instructions and guidelines, enough for us to catch the meaning of his words and be better as people. He even tells his disciples in the book of John:

> ***John 16:12–14***
> *¹² I have yet many things to say unto you, but ye cannot bear them now.*
> *¹³ Howbeit when he, the Spirit of truth, is come, he will guide you into all truth: for he shall not speak of himself; but whosoever he shall hear, that shall he speak: and he will show you things to come.*
> *¹⁴ He shall glorify me: for he shall receive of mine, and shall show it unto you.*

God never wanted us to be dependent on technology and a controlled civilization for survival and shelter. Even Christ himself walked on foot and lived off of the land. It is always important to remember the things you have heard about Christ. They will guide you to walking in spirit and in truth. God the father wanted the world to be completely dependent on him and themselves for survival. Many would argue that we have medicine, people live longer, we have cutting edge technology, and we can do more than we've ever done before. I would say yes, all that is true, but if life was truly meant to be this way, then why are we physically destroying planet earth? Why is the world as wicked and evil as it was before God sent the flood? Who are we to play God? Why does it already feel like we are already living in hell? Think about it, why would Freemasons, one of the most powerful organizations in the world, be sworn to secrecy by punishment of death if there wasn't something important they were hiding from you about history? They not only withhold knowledge, but those at the top degrees in Freemasonry are hiding the truth about who their knowledge comes from and the history of the fallen angels.

When I think about the Bible, I think, if I were a king or emperor, what would I gain by changing the Bible or by putting it together? The answer to that question is power. I thought about what I would want to change in the Bible from a political standpoint if I was in a rulers' shoes and wanted power. In history, kings and emperors looked at themselves as being chosen by the gods or as living gods themselves. Why wouldn't they believe that they could change anything in it? It is important to know that in those times the church was the law, and to go against the church was to go against God. When people say the Bible says follow the law of the land, I always think to myself, if people had done that through the years, most of us would be slaves, or worse, dead. Following the law of the land means a lot of times not following the laws of God; for example, the Bible says "thou shalt not kill," but because by law in the military you have permission to kill, you feel that it is alright. The law is what mankind is going to follow when they wage war against the people of God in the end. Even Christ in the Bible broke man's laws, or should I say traditions. The Bible even talks about evil being in high places and about how someone will give testimony against the rulers and kings of the world who are the makers of laws.

Mark 13:9

⁹ But take heed to yourself: for they shall deliver you up to councils; and in the synagogues ye shall be beaten: and ye shall be brought before rulers and kings for my sake, for a testimony against them.

The only laws I believe any man has to follow are the laws of God, not those of man. I also believe those in power would want to make sure people gave money to the church. None of this belongs to us; it belongs to God. If you think about it in the sense that God wanted us to live like Adam and Eve before eating the fruit, then money would have never existed. We would be completely dependent on God and ourselves. Another thing I think they would have also wanted to make people believe is that people can never make it to heaven without the church, that we can never truly understand the teachings of the Bible without a religious leader telling you what everything means. I guess people who don't live near a church are doomed, because a religious leader can't guide them into the arms of God. Some churches try to change and modernize the Bible and relate every message to something that might be happening in a person's life, when they should keep it basic. They add things to complicate the word when it is really so simple and the truth has never changed. My experience at church made me think about my friends from the hood. They almost never went to church, but they prayed a lot and could tell you almost any scripture from the Bible. I started wondering, did a man have to go to church to actually get the word? Many of the people in the Bible that God used didn't have a church home; they traveled preaching the gospel to those who would listen. I got this quote from a movie and I live by it because I believe it's true.

> **Stigmata**
> *The Kingdom of God is inside of you, and all around you, not in mansions of wood and stone, split a piece of wood I am there, lift a stone and you will find me. (http://m.imdb.com/title/tt0145531/quotes)*

I believe that God speaks to all of us through love and our hearts, and that everybody can have a direct connection with God without the help of another if they choose to. The spirit of God is all around us, and never leaves us not even for a moment. If you seek him, he will guide you to all that is righteous before the Father. I think that going to church is a great thing, whatever it takes to make a person better; it's good for prayer, it helps to renew faith, and it brings some hope. It is also a great place for worship and to give testimony to how good God has been to you. I believe in the Bible;

I just don't believe in the interpretations of everything understood by man. I am in no way against church or going to church; I still go, and I read my Bible a few times a week. I am only against the evil influence that has overcome most of the churches of today. I don't believe politics should ever be a part of the Bible or of the church. I believe that every man only has to answer to the authority of God and follow his commandments. I believe all of mankind should be free and every man or woman should have their God-given rights. Churches that are all about politics, money, and control and, in my eyes, are no different than the priest that had Christ crucified.

I have been to many churches in my lifetime and I have heard a lot of preachers talk about tithes, how the people should give the church money, because that was the only way God was going to bless them, telling people the only way God would fix all of their financial problems was if they gave to the church and that all those who didn't pay tithes were cursed. I wanted to stand up and tell those preachers that I was poor, that money and possessions really didn't mean anything to me, but instead, I remained seated and quiet. I thought to myself, if they truly are men of God, they don't have to preach about what a man should give, but trust and have faith that God will provide them and the church with everything needed. Back in the old times, preacher's preached and then had jobs during the week, but now they are paid a salary. I guess nowadays saving people and bringing them closer to God is a career; some would even call it a hustle. They collect money after every speaker, even in Sunday school. I guess if I want to make a couple extra bucks every week, I should become a minister. I know the church has bills, because even the church is enslaved and controlled by the laws of the world. I know that since most preachers don't work nowadays, they need for food and shelter, but they should not be in need of much.

Psalms 23:1
[1] The lord is my shepherd; I shall not want.

No man should care about money, but since society demands that we use it for survival, we do care. We should only use it if we have to until we learn not to have to anymore.

Matthew 5:3
³ Blessed are the poor in spirit: for theirs is the kingdom of heaven.

The reason the Bible says blessed are the poor in spirit is because those are the people who pay the real tithes. People have forgotten the purpose of tithes. The purpose was for those with increased goods, like food, to bring it to the storehouse so that the church could feed the poor. Tithes have always been for the purpose of helping the poor and less fortunate. A religious leader should not be living the American Dream, claiming it is in the name of God that they are blessed. In my opinion, the preacher should be the poorest person at church. They should always be trying to help people and should have complete faith in God for everything. I believe that a person's tithes should be given to anyone that needs help, whether it is to church or someone in need outside of church. Tithes don't have to always be what we call money; they don't have to be money at all. A piece of paper will not satisfy God. Especially when that piece of paper represents paganism, Satanism, strange gods, the Illuminati, and the protectors of everything represented on there, the Freemasons. Truthfully, I don't see how that can be offered as a righteous sacrifice to God, but it can be used to help people in a civilized world. I think you should give the church money to keep it open and to help people in need, but as far as offering something that represents evil to God, I don't think it is right. I thought to myself, if I had another offering besides money to offer the church, would they even accept it? I mean, the collection plate is so small, how can a bag of groceries fit? How much money you give to the church definitely does not reflect the outcome of anyone's blessings. If that was the case, all of those rich men who run the world and don't give anything would be broke. How much of your increased goods you give to the poor does reflect the outcome of your blessings, because I believe God will keep giving to you to help other people. The blessings you receive for having a kind heart and helping the less fortunate or anyone in need is far more valuable than anything on this earth. It is a blessing connected to your soul, not one of profit.

A lot of churches are out for money and teaching and misleading people; you should be watchful. Some churches have ATMs so they can make sure you have all your money for the collection plate. They run credit checks on the members. They have paid seats and members pay to sit up in the front. They pass the collection plate around a million times; you're broke before you leave. They ask you for how much they want you to give, saying things like, "I am going to start this offering off with a hundred and I want some saints to follow behind me." Some churches are made so big and beautiful and are worth millions. They have stained glass windows and a big screen projector, and they sell items out of church, trying to make a profit off its members. They sell dinners and holy water, have fashion shows, bookstores, and even built-in cafés. They are starting to sell some of everything in the church. What they are doing is no different from when Christ turned over the tables because people were selling things and exchanging money in the church. Preachers nowadays have their own private jets, golf courses, nice cars, and all the material things a man of God should not care about. I wonder, does the church now believe in saving money, spending big, making investments, growing financially, and keeping up with technology, and helping the helpless, the poor, the struggling, or the people less? You know we live in a cold world when not even some churches will help you nowadays. Most people don't see that they are blessed without having all of the things we think we need.

I think with everything that is going on in the world, church doors should stay open. I'm tired of the churches locking their doors. How could they be so worried about all the possessions on the inside when there are people on the outside who are cold, hungry, or in need of shelter? How can we live in a world like this and not have the church doors open around the clock? They could help so many people, help guide them in the right directions, but the greed of man even has its effects on the church. I think churches can do more to help people, instead of just trying to get more members to get more money and pretending to want to help people. Stop selling people dreams and show them the reality that God is truly with them during their time of need. Tithes can be anything that you give out of love to better the life of someone else less fortunate than you, and that includes time. There is no set percentage in giving increased goods to the poor. Whenever I see anyone in need, I feel obligated in my heart to help in any way if I can. Offering and dedicating your life to serving and being obedient is enough for God; having faith that God sees and knows all and will provide you with everything that you need. We should love our neighbors, show compassion to one another, and help each other in times of need. When you have increased goods, give to someone less fortunate. If everyone wealthy or better off than most helped somebody less fortunate than them, there wouldn't be people who are less fortunate. Everyone would be equal, the way we were supposed to be. If the church that you attend is a good one or changing for the better, offer them money to keep it open, and give tithes or whatever it may be to help the poor. That's how I live my life now and I couldn't be happier. In a perfect world, we would not need money and it would not rule our lives, but unfortunately, we don't live in a perfect world. So I would say use it if you absolutely have to until the day we no longer need it again. We should all start helping and loving each other. We worry too much about ourselves and what we have, when it is clear that we should be coming together in these times more than ever.

Instead, we keep each other at a distance and we sometimes even fear each other. I have even heard about and seen some religious leaders carrying firearms. They even have armed and unarmed security at churches nowadays. Those are men of little faith, because you should trust God to deliver you out of any situation or trust in his judgment.

Christ told Peter:

> **Matthew 26:51–52**
> *⁵¹ And, behold, one of them which were with Jesus stretched out his hand, and drew his sword, and struck a servant of the high priest's, and smote off his ear.*
> *⁵² Then said Jesus unto him, Put up again thy sword into his place: for all they that take the sword shall perish with the sword.*

My experience with church made me think that if churches weren't built the way they are, like palaces, would people even come to listen to the word? In this world today, would they follow a man that has stepped out on faith and just wants to teach the word of God? In my eyes, a man of God is not someone bound to the good in one religion, but someone that believes in the good in life and all things. What man is a true man of God who opens his heart to the good in one religion and does not admire the good in another? A true person in Christ opens his heart up to the good in every part of life. He is happy with what he has and he doesn't need much to be happy, a person who doesn't value money or material things; he values God, life, and his family. A person that even values and loves people they don't even know as God loves them. A person with a free mind, an open heart, a joyful spirit, and a clear soul, because through God all is forgiven. All you have to do is repent of your sins. Be a person who loves and cares for others with no thought of yourself. My heart is open to the good in everything, and I love and care for every living thing. I think some religious leaders need to take a long, hard look in the mirror and ask themselves, where is it I am preaching from, my heart or mind, my spirit or the flesh, that of God or that of the world? You can never be a true person of God until you have set yourself free of the prison that mankind has created through the knowledge left here by the fallen angels.

I don't believe in everything that is said to me by most religious leaders, but I have never just believed in everything anybody tells me. Most religious leaders are lost or are pretending to be men of God, quoting Bible scripture and deceiving people into following what they teach. I still pray for understanding after each lesson and pray that the words spoken by the speaker are of God and not of man. I grew up believing in the King James Version of the Bible and I used to attend a Pentecostal Church, but if there is another religion that I can find some good in, I acknowledge the good. I don't judge them on the other parts of their religious beliefs, because with all the churches I visited in my lifetime, including the one I attend now, I learned they are all flawed in some type of way. I can only pray that whatever people believe in, they find their way to the gates of heaven. Who am I to judge? I can only tell you what I believe, have observed, and have learned over the years and hope that you get something from it.

Even though my beliefs are different, I still believe there is something good I can take from other religions, like Buddhist monks: they practice patience, believe material things don't matter and in becoming one with themselves, and they have a different outlook on life. The Muslim Nation, they pray, fast, and show God his respect every day, no matter where they are in the world. Jehovah's Witnesses dedicate their time to spreading what they believe is the word to others and are not confined to a temple. The Baptist Church praises and worships the Lord together through dance and song. In the Catholic Church, some dedicate and give their lives up in service to God. In the Pentecostal Church, they believe that God forgives all through repenting for your sins. Even though Baptist, Catholic, and Pentecostal are Christian churches they all have their differences. I have not studied all of the beliefs of these religions. I don't know if any of these religions are of evil. All I know is the good things I named are all good qualities for any person to use if they believe in God. It is my belief that people of God shouldn't have to put a label on what they are; I don't really even believe in or truly have a religion. What is religion but another way to control people? I just believe in Christ and God the Father with all my heart and soul. I guess you would say I'm a Christian, because I believe in Christ, but any further than that, I have no label. I believe in living right, the good in life, in loving, and in doing right by others. I believe in truth and I am free from the deception and slavery of this world. I realized that the true church was inside of me, and I am learning to do God's will. I believe the elite have had an influence on all religion and government. My only hope is to understand and recognize the truth when I see it or hear it, the Gospel of the Kingdom, and to one day make it through the gates of heaven and stand before my creator. I believe Christ taught us to love each other no matter what race, shape, or size we are and to realize that life is what we make it and that any man can choose to be delivered from evil. I think that people should start to try to believe in the good in everything, pray for the bad, and hate sin. I believe the end is nearing and the seven seals have already begun to break. There is no doubt in my mind that the influence of Satan's followers is upon this earth. We can all choose to be delivered and keep our faith and not deny the name of Christ, our first love, until he returns. I would only pray that we can strengthen ourselves in the Gospel of the Kingdom, which is the truth, and stop letting the ways of the world influence our life and decisions.

Galatians 5:1
⁵ Stand fast therefore in the liberty wherewith Christ hath made us free, and be not entangled again with the yoke of bondage.

Christ came to set man free, as it was in the beginning, and man has brought the world back into slavery. Even though I believe his true message may be kept from us, I still believe it's written in our essences. I mean, think about it, why do you think they take every artifact and piece of literature created from the time and lock it up in a Vatican vault, away from the public's eyes? Never mind the Knights Templar, the people who started this, answering to the Pope, because every Pope has been a Freemason. Which means a big part of his job is keeping ancient knowledge a secret, even if it would change the world.

If you are offended by anything I have said in this chapter, it's probably because I am threatening your way of life in a civilized society. I hope that everything I have written causes you to do your own research and seek the truth for yourself. Now that we are completely controlled, they are taking steps to having absolute power and for the return of their god, Lucifer. Before I tell you how, you must remember that in government and war, nothing is what it seems, that you never really know the purpose or intent of the elite's actions until the damage has already been done, and even then it's just one big conspiracy.

CHAPTER 8

WARS AND RUMORS OF WARS

It was said the first time God was displeased with man he destroyed the world with water. This time it is said that the world will be destroyed by a lake of fire and that no man knows the date or time of Christ's return. However, the Bible does give very specific events leading up to his return. Everyone thinks that the end is near and that Satan is already walking the earth, only because we live in a world of chaos, that judgment day could be near and no man can hide from it. I have tried to look at all the facts, read Bible scripture, and look at history, hoping to find a sign of when the end is near. I believe that four out of the seven seals have been broken and Christ is warning us of his return. I believe that the attacks carried out by Osama Bin Laden were the breaking of the second seal.

> **Revelation 6:3–4**
> *³ And when he opened the second seal, I heard the second beast say, Come and see.*
> *⁴ And there went out another horse that was red: and power was given to him that sat thereon to take peace from earth, and that they should kill one another: and there was given unto him a great sword.*

Osama Bin Laden threatened to wage an Islamic holy war against the United States and its allies for its support of Israel.

He called for a Jihad against the Jews and all that support them in order to liberate Muslim holy lands from their grips. On September 11, 2001, a series of suicide attacks were carried out on the United States of America. Led by Osama Bin Laden, a man who was actually used, trained, funded, and created by the CIA, an alleged 19 Al-Qaeda terrorist members hijacked four commercial planes. They successfully took down the World Trade Center by crashing airplanes into each of the Twin Towers. Both of the World Trade Center Towers collapsed and crashed to the ground within two hours, destroying nearby buildings and businesses. The weird thing is the second tower that was hit was the Tower to collapse first. After both Towers collapsed, Building 7 also collapsed, but the crazy thing about Building 7 was it was never hit by a plane. They blamed the collapse of the two towers on the jet fuel from the planes, saying it melted the beams. It was later found that the jet fuel wasn't hot enough to melt the beams and that people on Ground Zero heard explosions before the Towers and Building 7 collapsed. Many believe that explosives were planted in the buildings, and that it may have been a controlled demolition. Especially since it was later found that Marvin Bush was the director of the electronic security company over the World Trade Center.

We will never know what really happened, because all of the evidence was quickly removed before any real investigation could be held. Then the melted beams were quickly sold to China, far away from the United States. The attack on the Twin Towers killed everyone on board of the planes, some rescuers, and many of the people who were working in the buildings. The third plane hijacked was crashed into the side of the in Arlington, Virginia. The jet that crashed and hit a section of the Pentagon hit a section that was under construction at the time. Even though they have footage of the plane crashing into the Pentagon, the plane they describe in the crash should have caused more damage to the building. The plane had a huge wingspan and the damage done to the building just doesn't add up to me. The fourth plane hijacked crashed to the ground in a field in rural Pennsylvania. Some of its passengers and flight crew attempted to retake control of the plane. It had been redirected towards Washington DC, and some say the hijackers' intentions were to crash the fourth plane into the White House. Nearly 3,000 victims lost their lives in the attack that brought America to its knees.

When I first found out about the terrorist attack, I was in school at the time. I think everyone in American remembers where they were when they first found out about the attack. My mother came to pick me up early from school that day. I remember getting home and watching the attacks on TV for the first time. Sitting there with my eyes glued to the TV screen as I watched the second plane crash into the Tower. I remember being in shock, thinking, is this really happening, as I watched the buildings crumble into nothing. Watching the news brokenhearted as people covered in dust were crying out for help, some hurt and lifeless, some people risking their own lives in hopes that they may save someone else's life. Then I remember the speech that President Bush gave about launching a war on terror and how America wouldn't stop until the terrorists at fault were brought to justice. I believe that day was the start of something more than just a war on terror. I believe that what happened in September of 2001 was just the beginning to a much bigger plan.

> **Matthew 24:7**
> *⁷ For nation shall rise against nation, and the kingdom against kingdom: and there shall famines, pestilences, and earthquakes, in divers places.*

After the attack, Bin Laden released a video saying that he was not at fault and that Israeli Zionists were at fault. Later, it was found that he was the man behind the attacks. After looking at all the facts, nobody really knows what happened on 9/11; we're just stuck with a bunch of conspiracy theories about what really happened. A few weeks after the attack, America invaded Afghanistan to dispose of the Taliban, who were accused of harboring the Al-Qaeda terrorists. They invaded Afghanistan to destroy their creation; after all, like I said before, the Al-Qaeda was created by the CIA. A few years later, Bush convinced America to invade Iraq in search of weapons of mass destruction. He explained that this was also an extension of America's War on Terror, even though he stopped looking for the man they told the world was responsible. That's if they ever were looking for him in the first place.

> **George Bush**
> *Who knows if he's hiding in some cave or not. We haven't heard from him in a long time. The idea of focusing on one person really indicates to me people don't understand the scope of the mission. Terror is bigger than one person. He's just a person who's been marginalized. I don't know where he is. I really just don't spend that much time on him, to be honest with you. (http:fair.org/blog/2011/05/02/ bushs-palpable-persistence-in-pursuit-of-bin-laden/)*

The weapons we invaded Iraq in search of were never found, and here it is almost 2012, and we're just now leaving Iraq. They did find Saddam Hussein, however, and he was held on trial and executed. All of those things were distractions for what they really invaded Iraq for. You see, in 2003 right after the invasion, men with earpieces broke into the museum. They blamed what happened to the museum on looters, but they knew exactly what they were looking for. Among the artifacts stolen were the ancient tablets the Sumerians left behind, probably filled with vital information they needed to be successful in taking over the world.

The United States mourned the death of all those people hurt and killed during the attack and the stock market stayed closed the week of the attack. When the stock market reopened, it recorded enormous losses, almost as big as the Great Depression, crippling and weakening the United States economy. A lot of people lost their lives as a result of the attack in 2001, including the United States soldiers fighting the War on Terror, the terrorists they were seeking, and even countless poor civilians in the Middle East. The point I am trying to make is that we will never know what really happened on 9/11. All we know is that the government knew about the attack before it happened, that some of the things that happened in the attack draw doubt on what really happened, and that it was covered up and quickly cleaned up. It doesn't matter if it was an inside job and the United States planned or allowed the attacks, if it was Israeli Zionists at fault and they really planned the attacks, if Bin Laden really did plan and carry out the attacks. In my eyes, they were all at fault and they could all have very much been working together. All I know is that the real goal was accomplished, and Osama Bin Laden was made out to be the villain in this story. Even though the story doesn't quite make sense, he was still blamed. That would make him the man that disturbed the peace on earth. He was the leader of Al-Qaeda and probably one of the most influential causes of the Islamic uprising in the Middle East.

You could also blame the attack for, not only the decline of America's economy, but the declining economies across the globe today. I believe September 11, 2001, was designed to create hatred against the Muslims, to replace leaders in the Middle East, to take away all of our privacy, to cause economics to begin to fail, and to reward those responsible for letting the attack happen. After all, our former President George W. Bush, the Saudi elite, corporate America, and European bankers made a fortune off of the attacks. When you sit at home and think about what life was like before September of 2001, you see a drastic change all across the world. The rich got richer and the poor got poorer. Even though Osama Bin Laden is a known terrorist leader, he acted as if he believed that the oppression that the Israelis were inflicting on Muslim/Arabs in the Middle East was wrong. That the support that other nations have for Israel is simply because they want to take control of the Temple Mount. He believed that in order to win the war against Israel, he would have to attack the main people supporting the

Israeli military, the United States. I mean, look at the places that were attacked during 9/11: the Pentagon, the World Trade Center, and the fourth jet allegedly was headed to Washington, DC. If you want to weaken a military, you hit its leaders and its finances.

Even though Osama Bin Laden may have planned and carried out an attack on the United States for its support of Israel, I still don't know what side he was on or whether this whole scenario was planned. I mean, politicians are like pro wrestlers; they pretend to be enemies to the public, but behind closed doors, they are really friends. When dealing with the elite, you have to assume every aspect of the situation. After all, George W. Bush and Osama Bin Laden's family have had business ties together. They're so close that right after the attack on America, the only planes that weren't grounded were the planes getting Bin Laden's family out of America to safety. The Bin Laden family and the Bush family are not enemies to each other. There is one thing I know about business and politics, and that's if it concerns you and the Bush family, it usually means you're part of the elite and part of the plan for the New World Order. Osama caused the economy to fall, and when the world needed leadership, President Bush took a vacation. At the end of his presidency, many thought that he did such a bad job, he even had two weapons of mass destruction thrown at him. A reporter took off both of his shoes and threw them at the head of former President Bush. He let the economy steadily decline to the point where America begged and welcomed with open arms the next step to the Illuminati's plan.

The War on Terrorism and the causalities from the war seemed endless and the breaker of the peace on earth was still at large. Al-Qaeda carried out many more attacks under the command of Osama Bin Laden across the world. Then, in 2008 I believe, the third seal was broken and he would bring balance before the war and until it was time for the economy to fail.

Revelation 6:5-6

⁵ And when he opened the third seal, I heard the third beast say, Come and see. And I beheld, and lo a black horse; and he that sat on him had a pair of balances in his hand.

⁶ And I heard a voice in the midst of the four beasts say, A measure of wheat for a penny, and three measures of barley for a penny; and see thou hurt not the oil and the wine.

In December of 2007, the United States of America went into a recession with George W. Bush in office. The economy was bad, a lot of people were jobless, and the unemployment rate was at an all-time high. The War on Terror was still an ongoing war and some started to believe that Bush was just after oil in the Middle East. The economy was in a recession, still trying to recover from the financial toll September 11 had on the country, and the never ending War on Terror America needed a savior, a man with the promise of change, and that would keep the economy balanced not make it better. On November 4, 2008, Democrat Barack Hussein Obama was elected the 44th president of the United States of America. I said Democrat, but it doesn't really matter what you are, because they are all part of the same plan and have the same agenda. The way George Bush, Sr., called for a New World Order is the same way Vice President Joe Biden and the leader of Iran called for it.

Barack Obama broke history by being the first black President of the United States. Even though many believe he is really the second black President. Remember, I told you that I believe there were presidents before George Washington; well, one of them was said to have been a black man. After Barack Obama was elected, Israeli forces moved into the Gaza Strip. Osama Bin Laden released a video celebrating the United States economic breakdown. He claimed that the attacks from September 11 weakened the United States' dominance and that United States support for Israel would also weaken. Bin Laden also called for a Jihad because of the Gaza attacks, urging the Muslim nations to come to the aid of its people.

The economic breakdown and the War on Terror were the first priorities of President Barack Obama's start in office.

After getting into office, Barack took a number of steps into helping out the economy, or should I say, keeping it balanced. In 2009, a stimulus bill was passed by the president called the American Recovery and Reinvestment Act. I don't know everything that was in that bill. The parts of the act that I did witness were when they gave first-time homeowners stimulus money back on their taxes to help banks. They extended unemployment benefits for jobless Americans. They gave out an incentive for people to get new cars by giving extra money towards the purchase of the cars to help the auto industry crisis. They also gave billions to the auto industry and banks to keep the economy from totally collapsing. The bill brought comfort to a lot of Americans, and the economy slowly began to balance out, and the United States was no longer in a recession. When the dust settled, people began to realize that there was no middle class America anymore, that it was only the rich and the poor, us versus them. Even though Obama may have done some good for the people, that doesn't mean that there isn't a catch. In the next chapter, I will show you why he is so important and how he set us up for death and imprisonment, but after helping the economy, there was only one thing left to do to restore the balance of the peace that was broken on earth. On May 1, 2011, the United States Obama Administration finally found Osama Bin Laden in a compound in Abbottabad, Pakistan. The fact that a known, wanted terrorist was in a mansion and not hiding in a bunker makes me think was he really never hiding at all. Osama was killed and his body was taken by the United States Navy special forces. Then, before anyone could see or identify the body, they dumped him overboard into the ocean. His death was celebrated across the United States as a victory, but was it really a victory? Did we get everyone responsible for the attack, did they really kill him, and were the things that were happening part of some bigger plan for a New World Order?

The second part of the third seal happened around the same time the 44th president was elected. The world food prices increased dramatically in 2007 and in the beginning of 2008, creating a world food price crisis. It's more than just a coincidence that the man who would not fix the problem but who would keep the economy balanced was elected the same time the world went into a world food price crisis.

Famine: an extreme scarcity of food (i.word.com.idictionary/famine)

In some countries the worldwide food crisis has already taken its toll. The United Nations believes that the global food crisis is due to the rise in oil and wine prices, the growth of biofuels, natural disasters, climate changes, and bad weather. The simple explanation is that the world is not producing enough food to feed the people who live on it. We are just halfway through the summer of 2012 now and experts are already reporting this year's drought as the worst we've seen in fifty years. The food scarcity is the cause of the soaring prices on food and the spreading hunger in the world. In many countries there have already been food protests and riots. The United Nations believes that the rise in prices has pushed an estimated 100 million people into poverty around the globe. Over the years, the price of food has increased by over 80% and people are struggling to buy food to feed themselves and their families. The United Nations is trying to come up with a solution to the global food crisis before it's too late. They believe that supporting farmers and sharing seeds with other countries will help. The food prices are at an all-time high and the UN is still trying to find ways to feed the hungry around the world. There is only the question of how they're going to do it and if we will ever see a decline in prices.

The real question I want to ask is, if the world is really in a food crisis, then why would they try to make a law stopping people from growing their own gardens at home? Why would they be arresting farmers for helping the poor and people in need? Are we really short on food or is this rise in prices just a way to push us further into poverty. Another major reason I believe this food crisis is happening is because of the collapsing population of bees across the world. The bees pollinate over 70% of crops, and without bees to pollinate the crops, some scientists believe the crops are dying. Scientists believe that the rapid decrease in the bee population is caused by the signals from cell phones. They claim the signals cause the bees to become lost and disoriented. Some of the bees never return to the hive; they just disappear. Another reason believed to be the cause of why bees are rapidly declining is insecticide. They believe chemicals used may be causing them to die off. We may never know all of the reasons the bees have begun to disappear, but here is a quote attributed to Albert Einstein's on the bee population.

Albert Einstein
If the bee disappears from the surface of the earth man would have no more than four years to live. (http://globalclimatechange.wordpress.com/2007/04/20/einstein-on-bees/)

I don't know if that's true or not, but if it is, mankind is in serious trouble. I believe the food shortage is also due to the massive amount of food governments around the world are stockpiling in bunkers. What are they preparing for? It's almost like they know something that we don't.

Many of the countries in the Middle East are without food and are hungry, and that is where there next plan unfolds. Some people believe that the United States' support of the Jewish people and Israel is because of their interest in oil and that the support of Israel ensures that the United States has an ally in the Middle East. That the United States' goal is to simply be able to dominate the Middle East due to the vast amount of oil reserves. Others believe that the support of Israel is an extension of America's War on Terror. I believe the support of Israel is because of Jerusalem. I believe it was never really about gaining oil and that the Illuminati may be just using oil prices to create poor living conditions for the world. They are pushing the world to its breaking point and stirring up hatred in the Middle East, between Muslims and Jewish Zionists. They are secretly planning World War III, the rebuilding of Solomon's Temple in Jerusalem, the rise of the antichrist and the false prophet, and a New World Order under their control. They are planning to imprison and kill all those who stand against them. I believe that what is going on in the Middle East is the breaking of the fourth seal.

> **Revelation 6:7–8**
> *⁷ And when he had opened the fourth seal, I heard the voice of the fourth beast say, Come and see*
> *⁸ And I looked, and behold a pale horse: and his name that sat on him was Death, and Hell followed with him. And power was given to them over the fourth part of the earth, to kill with sword, and with hunger, and with death and with the beasts of the earth.*

I believe that the fourth part of the world is the Middle East. The power has always been given to Israel in the Middle East, but now power is now being given to various Islamic Middle Eastern leaders. They are given the power to kill with weapons, hunger, and different technologically advanced machines used in times of war. The people that have been living in those various Middle Eastern countries are fighting against the oppression inflicted by its own and some foreign leaders. They are fighting to get those leaders replaced and are rising up. They are fighting for freedom. Still, I noticed something in those countries. Most of those leaders have been replaced with Islamic leaders, and I believe soon they will come together and go to war against Israel. Israel has diplomatic relationships with probably over a hundred nations across the globe. Israel is supported politically, militarily, economically, technologically, and by anti-Islamic countries. A large amount of the world politically supports Israel and their efforts to have complete control in the Middle East. The Israelis believe that the Jewish God condones their actions in the Middle East, as I am sure all Muslims believe their God does in the Middle East.

The war between Israel and Palestine has gone on for decades over the Holy Land. Israel believes that the Jewish people should have the rights to the Temple Mount. They believe it is the place God chose the divine presence to rest, where both of King Solomon's Temples were built, where God gathered dust to create man, and the place the Messiah will return to after they rebuild and create a third Solomon's Temple. Some Jewish people believe that the Temple Mount is the holiest of holy places and that the high priest could speak with God directly. Many Jewish people pray every day to be able to rebuild Solomon's Temple on the Temple Mount. There is just one problem: after the Muslim conquest of Jerusalem in 637 CE, Umayyad Caliphs commissioned the construction of the al-Aqsa Mosque and the Dome of the Rock, which is sitting where the Jews want to rebuild their Holy Temple. The Dome of the Rock is one of the Muslim community's holiest sites. Jerusalem used to be divided, and in June of 1967, the Israeli forces carried out a surprise attack on Egypt, Syria, Iraq, and Jordan. In the Six-Day War, Israel gained control of East Jerusalem and territories of more than three times their size. After the war, Israel made laws protecting the holy sites and offered citizenship to the Arabs under Israel's law. Palestine does not acknowledge Israel's right to exist and denies that the first two of Solomon's Temples were built on the Temple Mount, which is why war between them continues to this day.

Matthew 24:6
⁶And ye shall hear of wars and rumors of wars: see that ye be not troubled: for all these things must come to pass, but the end is not yet.

Countries all over the Middle East are using their power to kill people, cutting off food supplies, and causing prices to go so high people are starving. The killing in the Middle East seems endless, and when it says killing with "the beasts of the earth," it means tanks and different kinds of aircrafts, killer drones, guns, bombs, and whatever else that could be used to kill. I believe that what is going on in the Middle East is going to escalate into the third and last World War. They don't realize the force they hate most in this world is the same force that is arming them and bringing them together to go to war. I believe throughout history power has been given to the people of Israel, and they have made a lot of enemies over time, especially in the Islamic community. I believe power is now being given to the leaders of the countries who are rising up. Everywhere that a war has broken out, the leaders soon after have been replaced, because the people are tired of their living conditions. Fighting and protesting have broken out all over the Middle East. I believe as soon as they are done moving there pieces into place, something is going to happen in the Middle East where all Muslims will come together. After they call a Jihad, which means Muslims put their differences aside to go to war, they will go to war against Israel and its allies.

The elite control both sides of any war, and if any country is allowed to do anything, it is because it's what they want to happen. There is no doubt in my mind that what is now happening in the Middle East is somehow influenced by them. There are wars and rumors of wars. We have had troops fighting in Iraq and Afghanistan ever since the War on Terror. Fighting and protesting has broken out in countries all over the Middle East, such as Yemen, Jordan, Turkey, and Syria, in Russia and North Korea, and in countries in Africa especially, in Egypt and Libya. In many of these countries, they are supplying the same people they viewed as terrorists with weapons to wage a war. They are releasing known extremists who were imprisoned. Obama even just freed and traded the terrorist dream team for the release of one man. Then I thought about it: first, you create an uprising in the Islamic community. Then you give them the tools they need to start the war. Then you do something to keep pushing them to make them come together and want to go to war. Now that a little bit of time has passed, I think that ISIS may be the group to do it. They have a lot of the characteristics needed to cause the last World War. They are growing in numbers; parts of Africa have pledged their allegiance to them. The president is kind of pretending to care about them, but you can tell he is only doing enough so people won't question him but not enough to stop them from growing.

A few years back anti-American protests broken out all around American embassies all over the Middle East. As I said before, the Illuminati has always controlled both sides of war to ensure that their goal is carried out. Muslim groups with a deep hate for Israel are expanding to territories all over the Middle East, rapidly preparing for war. All the elite are doing is pushing both sides till they hate each other so much they just want to kill each other. The only question now is when the war will begin in these last days we are living in. I'm not able to keep up with everything that is going on in the Middle East, but the uprising in Egypt got national coverage. I watched it last year from time to time, but after what looked like a pale horseman appeared on TV in Egypt during the uprising, I knew that what was going on was real and that I should start being more watchful.

You see, what the Muslim community doesn't see is that it is their hate that will drive them to war and cause them to give up the very thing they are fighting for: the Temple Mount and freedom. If a war breaks out, there is no doubt in my mind that the Muslim holy lands in Jerusalem will be destroyed during the war. Any way it goes, Solomon's Temple will be rebuilt on the Temple Mount. The Freemasons are pushing for it to be rebuilt; the stone has already been cut, the blueprints have been drawn, and the architectural design of the third temple is ready. They have started calling Jews back to Jerusalem to prepare for the rebuilding. I don't believe the United States or any other nation really backs Israel because of oil, even though oil is essential to them in completing their plan for world domination. I believe they are planning the reconstruction of the temple, and the Illuminati are playing both sides to ensure a war and the world's economic collapse. Israel is now openly killing and bullying Muslim regions in the Middle East, and the Islamic community is rising up, killing themselves, and striking with acts of what would be viewed as terrorism against Israel and its supporters.

I ask myself a lot of questions about what is going on in the Middle East. Both sides are wrong. The Jews want to take the Temple Mount, and they are waiting for the opportunity to take it by force. The Islamic community wants to stop them through violent acts of destruction and wipe them out once and for all. I don't know exactly how the war will start or how all the dominoes will fall. I just know they are falling and all the countries in the Middle East and some parts of Africa will play a part in this upcoming war. Hopefully, they realize that it is a force playing both sides. Hopefully, they will stop and think about the big picture and how they will gain nothing by going to war but death. Hopefully, they realize that the war won't benefit them, but only a group of now many elite men who run and control the world. Remember, the Illuminati are like magicians; they create an illusion, and by the time you figure it out, they have already succeeded. Don't be that person in the crowd that likes the trick; be the one who questions it and calls it fake.

I believe the first four seals are connected. You see, apart they look as though they are random events that just happened throughout history. Together they look as though they are planned steps towards world domination taken by a group of men. Everything is connected and nothing is left by chance. In Revelation, John describes the horsemen by different colors. Is there a greater significance to describing different colors, because he already labels them by numbers. I believe John may have been describing the skin colors of the riders or describing what he is seeing in the seal. As for how long each of the seals lasts, the only time the Bible explains a set time for the seven seals is after the arrival and rise of the antichrist, but I will explain that later. The illusion they set is a little confusing, so let's strip it down so that you can see it even more clearly. Here is a quick recap on the first four seals and how they are connected.

A group of Luciferians named the Illuminati conquered the world and influenced government, religion, and everyday lives. The Illuminati is run by a powerful group of white men who are or pretend to be Jewish. Once you bow to their will, you are given a powerful position. It is important to know that the people given crowns in earlier times were kings or men of power. They have conquered almost everything and are now taking their final steps to completely ruling the world. Once they conquered everything, made us completely dependent on them, and it was almost time for the antichrist to come on the scene, the second seal became part of the illusion. Osama Bin Laden and the Al-Qaeda disturbed the peace on earth for the purpose of pushing the world into chaos and poverty, using fear to take away our privacy. The second horseman is red. Some people describe people in the Middle East as red skinned people, and this seal is also known as the fiery seal. John was describing what he saw in his dream in Revelation, so it could have been the way he viewed their skin or he could have been describing what happened. The attack damaged the economy, started the War on Terror, and gave the government a reason to legally take away all of our privacy rights (USA PATRIOT Act). It also gave banks a reason to take money out of circulation. The price of oil shot up and continues to raise the cost of living. The drop in the stock market also caused a lot of companies to go out of business or downsize in number of employees. It helped companies that they own gain a monopoly. It can also be connected directly to the housing crisis. After the attacks, violence grew around the world, and the War on Terror began and people were killing each other.

Once the world was on the brink of collapsing, then the third seal came along. A president comes along and restores the balance on earth and tries to come up with peaceful resolutions. He keeps the economy balanced but doesn't make it better, because soon, the economy will have to fail for the Illuminati to complete their goal. The third horseman is described as black. During the time Obama was elected, the world also went into a food price crisis. The Obama Administration sought out and killed Osama Bin Laden, further restoring the balance. He also balanced and aided other countries to keep them from collapsing, putting us in further debt. The price of oil is balancing out, but the poverty level and violence levels continue to rise. The fourth seal is described as the pale horseman. The fourth horseman is described as pale, meaning death. Israel and various Islamic Middle Eastern leaders are given power in the Middle East to kill and to cut off food supplies. The uprising now going on in the Middle East is because of hunger, poor living conditions, and the fact that they don't want someone else dictating what they do. All across the Middle East they are rising up and demanding that their leaders be replaced. Once those leaders are replaced, giving them the tools they need, the Illuminati will soon put the Jewish Zionists and the Islamic community against each other. After causing the third and last World War, which we already see signs of coming in the Middle East, they will create some type of social cataclysm, which will cause a global economic collapse.

It's only a matter of time before war breaks out in the Middle East. If there was to be a war in the Middle East, with our already crippled economy, that might just be the deciding factor in a global economic collapse, because oil prices would go through the roof. The reason that the first four seals' riders are connected is because they are all riding towards the same goal and are part of the same illusion: the rebuilding of Solomon's Temple in Jerusalem, the last World War, the rise of the antichrist and false prophet, and the New World Order.

CHAPTER 9

THE TIME OF PURIFICATION

In December of 2012, all of the planets in our solar system aligned in the middle of the Milky Way, creating a planetary alignment. This phenomenon happens about every 25,800 years. There were a lot of theories out there about what was going to happen around December 21, 2012. So many astronomical events happen at one time. Not only was everything aligned, but it was aligned in the center of our galaxy, a place known as the Dark Rift. This year, we also saw the transit of Venus; that's when Venus passes between the sun and the earth. There were three eclipses happening at one time during this event. It also marked an event that happens every year called the winter solstice; it occurs on December 21.

Along with this, we have experienced drastic changes to the weather and the climates around the world. The earth's poles have begun to shift and airports have had to offset their navigation systems. We are experiencing very strong solar storms, where the sun sends off solar flares, hitting the earth. The earth's magnetic field is also being pulled and twisted, weakening the field against those harmful solar flares and radiation. Some believe that those massive solar flares could cause a worldwide blackout, sending us back to the Stone Age. If enough solar flares hit earth, it could destroy the planet's atmosphere, killing every form of life on it. We have experienced a lot of earthquakes and other natural disasters. The icecaps have begun to melt and have caused the water levels in the oceans to rise all around the world. Some believed that alignment of the planets would have caused the earth's core to heat up and become unstable, destroying itself from the core. Some scientists believed that the earth could have had a rapid pole shift, and if it shifts too fast it would have caused major natural disasters. They believed that those natural disasters would have covered the earth, destroying almost, if not all, living things on this planet. Many people were worried that there might have been a super massive black hole in the middle of the Milky Way that could have possibly sucked earth in. There are many people who believe, and many ancient civilizations believed, there is another planet out there in our solar system, that this Planet X is unpredictable and could hit earth, destroying the atmosphere, or could come close enough to cause cataclysmic events.

It is because of these astronomical and strange events that people have begun to panic, wondering what is in store for us in the future. Many believed the world was going to come to an end in 2012 and they formed survival groups all around the world. Many people have different theories on what may happen to lead to the destruction of the earth. The Mayans predicted the alignment would happen on December 21, 2012, but why did their calendar end on that day, or does the calendar just start over?

Before I tell you what I believe, I want to look at the history of the Mayans and other parts of history that I feel are important to understanding and figuring out what we may be in store for in the near future. I believe that by understanding history we can figure out what happened in the past, what's happening in the present, and what we have in store for the future. We can understand the Gospel of the Kingdom and what God wants from us. We can also understand how Satan and his angels have deceived the world and had a major influence on our lives today. The only way to actually understand what may or may not happen in the future is by understanding the war between good and evil. I believe we were set up from the beginning and that everything that's happening in today's world has been the agenda since ancient times, since the beginning. Even though it seems like we may be doomed, I believe with all my heart that if we are headed down a path of destruction, these events can be stopped. The only way to stop them is by understanding the past to change the present for a better future.

The Mayan civilization was a culture of astronomy, architecture, mathematics, and science. It is said they discovered the planet alignments and predicted events using the equinoxes and Venus cycles. The Mayans worshipped many gods, but it is said that Kukulkan brought their laws, writing, agriculture, and medicine, and poured a vast amount of his knowledge into them. Kukulkan, known as the Serpent God, the Feathered Serpent, or the Plumed Serpent to the Mayans, was said to be a serpent in his natural form. The Mayans described Kukulkan as a white male, tall, with blazing blue eyes and long white hair. He was said to have come from the ocean on a raft of serpents. To the Mayans he was worshipped as their most important god. This Serpent God basically taught the Mayans everything they knew. He brought advancements to their civilization and added to their way of life. Then it is said that he returned to the ocean, telling the Mayan people that one day he would return.

The temple of Kukulkan is located in the jungles of Chich'en Itza, an ancient Mayan city in Central America. The temple is a four-sided pyramid and the entire structure is a three-dimensional calendar. The architecture of the temple was built to have a strategic orientation to the sun. During the spring and the fall equinoxes every year, a shadow appears on the steps of the north side of the temple resembling a serpent going down into the underworld and then its head appears to come out of the ground. The serpent's head is at the base of the pyramid. There were 91 steps on each side and the top platform, which represented 365 days of the year. The Mayan calendar is even more accurate than the Gregorian calendar that we use today. I believe that through the teachings of the Serpent God the Mayan culture began to have rituals to

THE TIME OF PURIFICATION

please the gods. They would have ceremonies where they cut out the hearts of children, women, slaves, or prisoners of war to anoint the idols with fresh blood. The people being sacrificed would be painted blue and held down on a stone table by their hands and feet. They would have their chests cut open with a stone knife and their hearts snatched from their bodies. After anointing the idols, the hearts of the sacrificed were thrown into an open pit of fire and sometimes eaten. They believed that through these rituals and ceremonies, the sun gained its substance and that it pleased the gods. The Mayans also believed that the only people who went to heaven were children who died at birth and people who were sacrificed. Everyone else went to the underworld and had to make it past sinister gods in order to make it into heaven.

Then in the 1500s the Spanish conquistador Hernán Cortés arrived and the Aztec people mistook them as the second coming of their Serpent God. We know the Spanish conquistador traveled to Mayan lands and saw the Mayan culture as demonic and evil. They burned almost all the history of the Mayans. We don't know what was in the codices that they burned, but there were only four codices saved. I wonder what was so important about those four that they were saved? They were taken to Europe to be studied and translated. Even with the codices and all the hieroglyphs in the temple, it's still hardly enough information to know about the whole Mayan civilization.

After learning a little bit about the Mayan people, I started asking myself questions about their history. The first thing I asked myself was, why was there a giant serpent coming down the side of the Mayan temple to the north and why did it look as though it went down into the underworld but then came back up? When the Bible speaks of Lucifer and refers to his throne, it refers to the north. Just look at Christmas; for example, we celebrate the birth of Christ, but on the other hand, we also have Santa Claus. He dresses up in all red, comes from the North Pole bearing gifts, and his name scrambled is Satan Lucas. The devil hates any celebration of Christ, but still, Satan, I mean Santa, comes from the north. When the devil is cast out of heaven for his pride and rebellion against God, the Bible talks about the north.

> **Isaiah 14:12-15**
> ¹² How art thou fall from heaven, O Lucifer, son of the morning! how art thou cut down to the ground, which didst weaken the nations!
> ¹³ For thou hast said in thine heart, I will ascend into heaven, I will exalt my throne above the stars of God: I will sit also upon the mount of the congregation, in the sides of the north!
> ¹⁴ I will ascend above the heights of the clouds: I will be like the most High.
> ¹⁵ Yet thou shalt be brought down to hell, to the sides of the pit.

I believe the Serpent God Kukulkan and the serpent that came to Eve and convinced her to eat of the forbidden fruit maybe one and the same. The acts of the Mayans and their culture just seem wrong and evil to me. I believe, as the Spanish believed, that the practices, rituals, and ceremonies in the Mayan culture were evil. I believe the Mayan Serpent God was actually Lucifer himself during his travels. I believe after Christ came and died for our sins, the devil knew he had a little bit of time left. So he poured as much knowledge into the civilizations away from Christianity as he could. I believe he may have stayed with the Mayan people until after the temple was built and the codices were created or until he was confident enough that they could create these things on their own. He taught the Mayans to commit the evil acts and rituals they were doing. The sacrifice of people to please the Serpent God, believing it would nurture and please the gods, is just evil.

The point is, the Serpent God is constantly known in history as the bringer of knowledge to civilizations. The Illuminati believes that through knowledge, technology, power, control, and by perfecting themselves in witchcraft, sorcery, or a higher consciousness they, too, can become gods. If fallen angels taught civilizations knowledge about science, math, astronomy, astrology, and how to write, that would mean that the technologies and all the advancements we see today may be from what they left behind. That also means that this world's advancements may have been planned from the moment Adam and Eve sinned in the beginning. I'm not saying knowledge is evil or good, and now that we have grown in knowledge and have technology, it is here to stay. I'm just saying, what if God knew the nature of man and wanted to keep things simple. I mean, think about it. We have this big brain, but the average human only uses 10% of it. Maybe Lucifer tried to make man too intelligent and God only allowed us to access a small part of our brain.

Think about the oldest bones ever found on earth. This is where science pulls the theory of evolution, that mankind evolved from apes. It's because Lucy, the oldest humanoid bones found at the time, was said to have walked upright, been hairy, not needed clothes, and had a much smaller brain. Science concluded that she must have been in-between a human and an ape, which is why she is known as a humanoid. If she was before us, then that must have been how God created us, so why are we so different now? For the answer I urge you to look at the medical symbol, the book of Genesis, and what ancient civilizations said about what happened. The medical symbol is two serpents wrapped around a staff resembling DNA, with angel wings at the top. The book of Genesis says that after eating the forbidden fruit, Adam and Eve realized they were naked. Is it because they lost the hair their bodies were covered in? Then it says they started to think differently as if they suddenly started to accesses more of their brains. Then ancient civilizations say that the beings that fell from the sky altered mankind's DNA. Are all of these stories one in the same? Is that why the Bible tells us sin passes on, because we have the blood of our fathers? I don't know, but all of the stories sound similar. When people speak of the third eye, it refers to the pineal gland, because that is the only other part of your brain that has retinas like your eyes. Many believe by learning how to access it, man can unlock the other parts of the brain, and they themselves can become gods. That is why those in control always take pictures covering one eye. They believe that man can do as he pleases, because man himself can become a god by accessing all of his brain.

Even though ancient civilizations claim their knowledge came from a serpent, all things come from God. So I believe knowledge can be a gift, but it is one that mankind has obviously abused and one we may have never been meant to have. Some of the great inventions we take claim for today were already invented by ancient civilizations, and some things they knew how to do are still a mystery to us today. If you look hard enough, you will find that most of the great inventors studied ancient knowledge, were part of the occult, were in fraternities or secret organizations, or studied the mystery religions. I believe Lucifer convinced ancient civilizations to leave information, knowledge, and clues as to his return. King Solomon may have been the key to mankind understanding what fallen angels left behind after the mysterious disappearance of some ancient civilizations. What the Templars found under his temple may have given the elite the upper hand, the power to carry out a plan and control the world over a period of time. All of that made me think about the G in the middle of the Freemason symbol. God is the creator, but who do they view as the Grand Architect behind the design of this world?

The degrees in Freemasonry and the names of their lodges are nothing more than history lessons. Once you've followed the light to the top degree, if you are chosen to join that inner circle in Freemasonry, that is when they let you know that the light bearer of the light you've been following is in fact Lucifer. That it is your duty to protect the real history and knowledge of this earth. I believe the hieroglyphs of these ancient civilizations are the key to unlocking the history of the fallen angels. I believe Lucifer convinced ancient civilizations to unknowingly create detailed codices, hieroglyphs, and cornerstones. They left behind organized timelines of future events, explaining steps to prepare things that would have to happen in order to prepare for the antichrist, the false prophet, and Lucifer's return. Satan's deception was more than just him talking people into committing evil acts that pleased him or telling Eve to bite a piece of fruit. He left behind knowledge that, with time, when understood and in the wrong hands, could be used to push the world into continuous evil again. I believe the Illuminati have used knowledge to influence the world, have control over civilizations today, and have a major influence or control over all religion. We know from the Bible that Satan walked the earth and he deceived the nations until he was cast into a bottomless pit for a thousand years.

Revelations 20:1-6

¹ And I saw an angel come down from heaven, having the key of the bottomless pit and a great chain in his hand.

² And he laid hold on the dragon, that old serpent, which is the Devil, and Satan, and bound him a thousand years.

³ And cast him into a bottomless pit, and shut him up, and set a seal upon him, that he should deceive the nations no more, till the thousand years should be fulfilled: and after that he must be loosed a little season.

⁴ And I saw thrones, and they sat upon them, and judgment was given unto them: and I saw the souls of them that were beheaded for the witness of Jesus, and for the word of God, and which had not worshipped the beast, neither his image, neither had received the mark upon their foreheads, or in their hands; and they lived and reigned with Christ a thousand years.

⁵ But the rest of the dead lived not again until the thousand years were finished. This is the first resurrection.

⁶ Blessed the holy is he that hath part in the first

> *resurrection: on such the second death hath no power, but they shall be priest of God and Christ, and shall reign with him a thousand years.*

Most people believe that Lucifer is now walking the earth and that his thousand years of being locked away starts when Christ returns, but in the Bible, in the end, it clearly says that the beast is released from the bottomless pit. Plus, in history, Lucifer didn't hide in the shadows from man; he presented himself as a god and as the light. That is why I believe Satan was already cast down into a bottomless pit, until the seventh seal is broken and the fifth trumpet has sounded. While Satan is there, he cannot speak or deceive and influence man with his words. When Christ returns, those who did not take the mark, who repented, who spoke the word of God, and who were righteous will go with Christ for a thousand years. That is when the beast will be released from the bottomless pit, not when he will enter it.

I believe that all the information that these ancient civilizations left behind was for a purpose and designed to make the world what it is today. So people would sin and praise and worship the beast. The first time God destroyed the world, it was because of the deception of Satan. Now it is because those that follow Satan's teachings deceive the world, and it is now the deception of man. I believe just as God left us Revelation and the Bible warning us of Christ's return and the things that would happen in the end of days, the Illuminati have precisely carried out and followed the directions left behind by Lucifer. They are doing exactly what is written in Revelation, because they know most people will watch but do nothing. They will chalk it up to end time prophecies and say, well, that's what is supposed to happen. They completely control, dominate, and influence the world's decisions. Many people fear the thought of being called crazy, they fear prison, they fear death, among many other things. That is why they are afraid to stand up for what is right.

THE TIME OF PURIFICATION

> **Luke 12:4**
> *⁴ I tell you, my friends, do not be afraid of those who kill the body and after that can do no more.*

Many of the ancient civilizations that built great pyramids and temples left artifacts behind that speak of many things. One of those things is what some people have come to call doomsday, which was expected to happen December 21, 2012, but what do the Mayans say and describe happening? They say it will be a time of transformation and rebirth, the start of a new era; they believe it will be a time of purification and that the god of destruction will return to his temple. They also say that we will have three days of darkness. I believe that the Mayan people weren't describing the end of the world, or doomsday, but that they may have been describing something worse. Let's take a look at what the Bible says that is similar to what the Mayans believed. I believe that during the upcoming war, the antichrist will suffer a deadly wound, and that's when the antichrist, who is the god of destruction to the Mayans, will go to the holy land and proclaim himself God and deceive the world.

> **Revelation 13:3–5**
> *³ And I saw one of his heads as it were wounded to death; and his deadly wound was healed: and all the world wondered after the beast.*
> *⁴ And they worshipped the dragon which gave power unto the beast: and they worshipped the beast, saying, Who is like unto the beast? who is able to make war with him?*
> *⁵ And there was given unto him a mouth speaking great things and blasphemies; and power was given unto him to continue forty and two months.*

I believe that the antichrist will promote himself to the world after this year's alignment, as a bringer of peace after chaos breaks out everywhere. I believe he will wait a few years, though, because doing it right after the alignment would draw too many red flags in the eyes of man. When it comes to ancient civilizations, we know that the alignment of the stars and planets was very important. They described it as the time they could communicate with the gods or when the gods manifested themselves into the leaders of civilizations. I believe that may have been what the Great Pyramid was used for in ancient times. The three days of darkness I am not sure about; only time will tell, but maybe the three days of darkness are because of the winter solstice. It could also be talking about the three eclipses earth will have during the galactic alignment. After the war, I believe the antichrist and false prophet will come up with a seven-year peace treaty and they will rise to power. This peace treaty will not only stop the war but end hunger on earth. The Bible says when these things happen, blessed are those who can last three and a half years. It also says the antichrist will have power for three and a half years.

During my research, I also found that in the month of December pagan worshippers celebrate a holiday. The winter solstice, also known as Yule, is the celebration of the rebirth of the unconquered sun. It is also the birth and rebirth of the pagan sun god Horus. Horus was said to have had a lot of similarities to Christ, but I really couldn't find many similarities between them. I also happen to know that Horus was Lucifer himself, the sun god. After studying a little bit about pagan gods who were said to be like Christ, I found that none were even close to being like him. They were designed to make Christ look as though he was a copycat. Lucifer knew why Christ was going to be born on earth to die for our sins, and he would do anything to get you to not believe in him. Another thing that makes people skeptical is the fact that many believe that when Christmas was formed, it may have been because the winter solstice fell on December 25th that year, that the celebration of Christmas may be because of Horus and is in fact a pagan holiday. If you ask me, every holiday we celebrate is pagan. Nobody truly

THE TIME OF PURIFICATION

knows when Christ was born, and it is because of that fact that I celebrate the birth of my savior every day.

Looking into the history of Christmas is just one big conspiracy. I believe that some of rituals done on Christmas may have some pagan origins. I no longer celebrate Christmas, but since I was raised to believe that was the day Christ was born, I still acknowledge that it may have been the day he was born, because we still really don't know. I believe Christ was the Son of God and had no connection to Horus or any other pagan god whatsoever. Even though I see no clear connection between Christ and any of the pagan gods spoken of in history, I believe that there could be a connection between Horus, Lucifer, and the antichrist. The winter solstice happened to fall on the same day as the planetary alignment in 2012. The ancients believed that pagan gods could manifest themselves into man during planetary alignments, and because of that day being Yule and being celebrated as the rebirth of the unconquered sun, I believe the antichrist is here. I believe that the stories of Horus and other pagan gods in history and the actions of the enslaved churches nowadays will play a critical role in creating blasphemies against the church in the end. In the Bible, the last World War paves the way for the antichrist, who I believe is already here; the war gives birth to his rule on earth.

The Mayans also describe the time after December 21, 2012, as the time of purification, but what does the book of Daniel say about the end times and the time of being purified?

Daniel 12:10–12

¹⁰ Many shall be purified, and made white, and tried; but the wicked shall do wickedly: and none of the wicked shall understand; but the wise shall understand.

¹¹ And from the time that the daily sacrifice shall be taken away, and the abomination that maketh desolate set up, there shall be a thousand two hundred and ninety days.

¹² *Blessed is he that waiteth, and cometh to the thousand three hundred and five and thirty days.*

The time of purification is the time that the world realizes the truth about this world, the time that the world stands up to the evil that controls this world, and before you read the next chapter, you must understand the world is going to hate you, and those close to you, family, strangers, whoever you may speak the truth to, are not going to understand. The world's beliefs have a hold on them and it is a burden that you will have to live with, knowing the truth and not being able to save the souls of the people closest to you.

2 Thessalonians 2:1–17

¹ Now we beseech you brethren, by the coming of our Lord Jesus Christ, and by the gathering together unto him,

² That ye be not soon shaken in mind, or be troubled, neither in spirit, nor by word, nor by letter as from us, as that the day of Christ is at hand.

³ Let no man deceive you by any means: for that day shall not come, except there come a falling away first, and that man of sin be revealed, the son of perdition;

⁴ Who opposeth and exalteth himself above all that is called God, or that is worshipped; so that he as God sitteth in the temple of God, shewing himself that he is God.

⁵ Remember ye not, that when I was yet with you, I told you these things?

⁶ And now ye know what withholdeth that he might be revealed in his time.

⁷ For the mystery of iniquity doth already work: only he who now letteth will let, until he be taken out of the way.

⁸ And then shall that wicked be revealed, whom the Lord shall consume with the spirit of his mouth, and shall destroy with the brightness of his coming:

⁹ Even him, whose coming is after the working of Satan with all power and signs and lying wonders,

¹⁰ And with all deceivableness of unrighteousness in them that perish, because they received not the love of the truth, that they might be saved.

¹¹ And for this cause God shall send them strong delusion, that they should believe a lie:

¹² That they all might be damned who believed not the truth, but had pleasure in unrighteousness.

¹³ But we are bound to give thanks always to God for you, brethren beloved of the Lord, because God from the beginning chosen you to salvation through sanctification of Spirit and belief of the truth:

¹⁴ Whereunto he called you by our Gospel, to obtaining of the glory of our Lord Jesus Christ.

¹⁵ Therefore, brethren, stand fast, and hold the traditions which ye have been taught, whether by word, or our epistle.

¹⁶ Now our Lord Jesus Christ himself, and God, even our Father, which hath loved us, and hath given us everlasting consolation and good hope through grace,

¹⁷ Comfort your hearts and stablish you in every good word and work.

CHAPTER 10

THE FALL

In the near future, I am sorry to say, mankind, society, and this generation will fail. Fear is going to get the best of man and it is going to cause the world to hate those who they wrongfully believe are at fault. They are setting us up for a New World Order under the rule of the antichrist. It doesn't matter whether they are Democrats, Republicans, president, vice president, king, or queen. All of the world's leaders are calling for a one-world government. If you still don't believe that everything that is going on in the world is planned, one of the world's most powerful Freemasons in history, General Albert Pike, gave us a heads-up with this letter. He was a known Lucifer worshipper, a Master Mason, some say the leader of the Ku Klux Klan, and a member of the Illuminati. He describes how they will actually carry out their plans.

> **Albert Pike**
> *The Third World War must be fomented by taking advantage of the differences caused by the "agentur" of the "Illuminati" between the political Zionists and the leaders of Islamic World. The war must be conducted in such a way that Islam (the Moslem Arabic World) and political Zionism (the State of Israel) mutually destroy each other. Meanwhile the other nations, once more divided on this issue will be*

> *constrained to fight to the point of complete physical, moral, spiritual and economical exhaustion ... We shall unleash the Nihilists and the atheists, and we shall provoke a formidable social cataclysm which in all its horror will show clearly to the nations the effect of absolute atheism, origin of savagery and of the most bloody turmoil. Then everywhere, the citizens, obliged to defend themselves against the world minority of revolutionaries, will exterminate those destroyers of civilization, and the multitude, disillusioned with Christianity, whose deistic spirits will from that moment be without compass or direction, anxious for an ideal, but without knowing where to render its adoration, will receive the true light through the universal manifestation of the pure doctrine of Lucifer, brought finally out in the public view. This manifestation will result from the general reactionary movement which will follow the destruction of Christianity and atheism, both conquered and exterminated at the same time. (http://www.threeworldwars.com/albert-pike2.htm)*

If General Albert Pike did in fact write this, it would mean this would have had to have been written in the 1800s. Now think about what is happening in the world today. This confirms that everything I described to you is leading up to this. The debt system, what happened on September 11, 2001, all the actions of our current president, and everything else going on in the world is not by chance and has been an organized plan for a very long time. Even more than the Islamic community rising up, the world is rising up, and protesting for better living conditions has broken out everywhere. People are tired, mentally, physically, and spiritually, and they are definitely tired of the economic status. Some have hope that things will get better, but sorry to say, it is only going to get worse, unless we change together, as a whole. The Illuminati have engineered our global economic collapse and they will blame what happens on the revolutionaries and those who read and believe in the truth. There is nothing we can do to stop it unless the world changes. If not, we can only plan to survive. The now balanced economy and oil prices tell me that almost anything could trigger the complete failure of economies across the globe. The Bible speaks of something happening before or around the same time the war breaks out, before people turn on each other, before the antichrist and false prophet rise to power, and before the economy collapses. Before the fifth seal is broken, the Gospel of the Kingdom must first be published and preached around the world.

> **Matthew 24:14**
>
> ¹⁴ *And this gospel of the kingdom shall be preached in all the world for a witness unto all nations; and then shall the end come.*
>
> **Mark 13:10**
>
> ¹⁰ *And the Gospel must first be published among all nations.*

This world cannot end without you knowing the truth, without you being given the option to choose sides. After the Gospel is preached and people know the truth, many people are going to turn on each other more than they have already been doing. It is because most people already serve fallen angels or have lived in slavery so long that they are not ready to be freed. Their minds can't handle the truth or the fact that they have been living a lie. Some people are so used to being slaves that they will fight to protect the system or the people who have enslaved their minds. They will see the world for what it really is and recognize truth from deception, and they will choose deception because they cannot function without being controlled. To them, deception is easier than facing the truth. Around this same time, when people began to really turn on each other, I believe the third and last World War will begin in the Middle East. All around the world, people will be lost, and there will be more famine and a scarcity of food and clean water. People will fight over food and water, even kill for it.

> *Mark 13:12-13*
> *12 Now the brother shall betray the brother to death, and the father the son; and children shall rise up against their parents, and shall cause them to be put to death.*
> *13 And ye shall be hated of all men for my name's sake: but he that shall endure unto the end, the same shall be saved.*

Those who choose deception will turn on those who realize the truth. They will blame the fact that they can't live a normal, civilized life with the most basic of things on those who believe in living the way God intended man to live and those who speak the truth. Economies will fail all around the world. People will panic, and that's when the Illuminati will rise to power. During the war and the failure of the economy, everything is going to be so bad, people are going to need something or someone to believe in. The very next step comes from the book of Matthew:

> *Matthew 24:23-24*
> *23 Then if any man shall say unto you, Lo, here is Christ, or there; believe it not.*
> *24 For there shall arise false Christ, and false prophets, and shall show great signs and wonders; insomuch that, if it were possible, they shall deceive the very elect.*

This is how they will create order out of chaos after the war. I believe the antichrist will create a world peace treaty with equal rights for all. The antichrist will have Solomon's Temple rebuilt for the third time. He will come up with a solution to the world's problems by feeding the hungry, giving drink to those who are thirsty, and by ending poverty. That's probably why governments around the world have been working so hard to store food and supplies in underground bunkers. They will make it seem as though the only solution to the problem is to unite all the world's governments and to accept the mark of the beast, which will grant them absolute control over people. Once they unite the governments, it will go from just giving away food and supplies to helping people, to demanding your allegiance to get the basic things you need. Demanding your loyalty for rewarding you and your family with the basic things you need in a civilized world. Saying that by taking a chip in your arm or forehead, it will prevent all crime and create peace on earth.

This generation is so important to them completing their plan, because we don't do anything ourselves anymore. We are almost completely dependent on technology for survival. We are lazy and they will use that to their advantage. How do you take over the world and have one-world government? First, you establish a system that gives you power and control. Then you use fear to take away people's privacy. Make people's living conditions bad. Create one bad situation after another, raising the price of oil and giving banks a reason to take money out of circulation. Influence the world to be in poverty then watch and let the already brainwashed society become weaker. Let them destroy each other, because the moment things get bad, a brainwashed society is sure to turn violent, to rob, steal, and kill. Make it so violence is the only thing people hear or think about. Promote the violence through TV and radio so that the civilized society you control will beg for the government to step in to take control of everything around us to keep us safe. To bring security to the world so people feel safe again. Use fear to push laws into existence, preparing for the New World Order.

A few words of what Albert Pike wrote make me wonder if slavery and the racial tension between black and white people in America was for a purpose. I mean, just think about it. Take a man of color and enslave him and his family; beat them, rape them, break their minds. After a few years, give them a little freedom, but keep them poor and uneducated and unequal; make them wish they had rights, make them dream of a better life, make them think they freed themselves when really freeing them is the biggest part of them being slaves. Financially back their movement to be free (Jacob Schiff, NAACP) then free them but kill their leaders. Sacrifice every president who played a part in giving them their freedom to conceal the secret. To train those oppressed to riot and fight, because they know how useful it would be in the future. Abraham Lincoln and JFK were probably assassinated by the same group of people who were found guilty of assassinating Martin Luther King, Jr., in 1999. Keep them in poverty and let us choose who among them will be rewarded with worldly possessions, only to push our philosophy and our laws, to promote violence, and to brainwash all those who look up to them for the material possessions we have given them. They will be the biggest believers and promoters of Lucifer's philosophy. They will think money is everything and they will treat the rich like gods and the poor like nothing. They will judge people by material possessions, never realizing they are equal, never to be happy with what they have, and believing money is key. They will kill, steal, and ultimately, destroy each other over a piece of paper worth nothing. We need them to turn violent, because in that day, when it is clear to the world it is out of control, we will declare martial law and gain absolute power, which has always been the plan.

This is why they have killed all those black youth and set the murderers free. It gave them a reason to transport all the tanks and weapons to every major city. It caused the awakening movement, which follows the Luciferianism philosophy and also promotes black power. Well, whether it's black power or white power, it's still racist and hateful. It also promoted black violence and brought us one step closer to martial law. They knew we would riot, loot, come together, and stand up against them; it's what they trained us to do in the 60s. Anytime they want black people to come together for a revolution, they know exactly what to do. Slavery has always been a part of history, but the leader of the KKK, Pike, writing this in the 1800s, makes me think we were slaves for this purpose and freed only to be slaves to something else, new slaves to their cause and society. The gun stores are already recording record sales of firearms, because people fear one day they might have to protect their families. The Illuminati control all forms of government and religion to keep people from ever knowing the truth. They influence religion by making sure its leaders can quote the Bible well, but then teach them part of the truth, worldly beliefs, and influence them to move further away from God's plan for mankind. They have taught those beliefs over the years, so that it is a firm belief among most religious leaders, so that they will teach their followers the same beliefs and lies.

> **2 Corinthians 11:14–15**
> *¹⁴ And no marvel; for Satan himself is transformed into an angel of light.*
> *¹⁵ Therefore it is no great thing if his ministers also be transformed as the ministers of righteousness; whose end shall be according to their works.*

Even during these troubled times, people will feel as though they can't even turn to church for help. Many will be lost, and some will just be glad that someone came up with a solution to the problem. False apostles and prophets are ready and have been in the churches for years, and according to some of my sources, they have been influencing and investing in religion since the Illuminati formed. I have even witnessed it for myself, as a matter of fact. There hasn't been a church I have been to in the last couple of years that hasn't had a religious leader claiming to be a prophet, and I have found them all to be false. Even without what my sources informed me of, I see it more now today than ever before, and now that I know the truth, I can see them more each day. When the antichrist arrives, he will speak blasphemies about the church and God's people because of things the Illuminati have secretly influenced the church on throughout the years. Even the good and righteous will become enemies to the world. The antichrist will get the world to believe that we are the cause of the world's downfall. That he is the way and that we should worship him.

THE FALL

> **Revelations 13:6-10**
>
> ⁶ *And he opened his mouth in blasphemy against God, to blaspheme his name, and his tabernacle, and them that dwell in heaven.*
>
> ⁷ *And it was given unto him to make war with the saints, and to overcome them: and power was given to him over all kindreds, and tongues, and nations.*
>
> ⁸ *And all that dwell upon the earth shall worship him, whose names are not written in the book of life of the Lamb slain from the foundation of the world.*
>
> ⁹ *If any man have an ear, let him hear.*
>
> ¹⁰ *He that leadeth into captivity shall go into captivity: he that killeth with the sword must be killed with the sword. Here is the patience and the faith of the saints.*

The only reason they will be able to speak blasphemy against the church is because we have allowed them to corrupt most of the tabernacles of God today. We have become slaves again and have forgotten our first love, Christ, and all that he has taught us about how to walk in spirit and in truth. They will use that against us to try to corrupt the minds of many.

When the antichrist arrives on the scene, he will convince people that if they are not with him, they are against the New World Order. The false messiah will have Solomon's Temple rebuilt in the Middle East and the antichrist will prey on the weak and proclaim himself as God and a savior of the people. Many people will be fooled and believe in his miracles and his words. Many are awaiting his arrival and will believe he is truly the Messiah. I don't know who he is, but I will know when the time comes. We all will, but sadly, many will still choose him. During these times, God will send messengers to help man see the truth, messengers to stand against everything that is now happening in the world today.

Many people will rise against the antichrist and those who believe in Lucifer's philosophy. Those who hear the truth and are faithful will rise up and speak out against them, and they will answer with violence. The United States has already allegedly ordered 30,000 guillotines to behead those who truly believe in God and stand for what's right. The antichrist will have power over the world's militaries, every armed government-based company, and people who want to join his army to bring order to a world in chaos. A lot of the people who stand against them will be killed or imprisoned. To those who are armed soldiers, who are already in the military, or to those men in cities who are in uniform, remember, if you lead into captivity, you will be imprisoned, and if you kill innocent people, then you will suffer the same fate. Martyrs are people that get killed for their religious or other beliefs. The Illuminati will wage a war against those who recognize the truth, who no longer want to be slaves to their system.

I believe in the near future, people will begin to repent for their sins and speak out the truth about life, what is now happening in the world, and the good news of the Kingdom. They will start to live free and they will blame those who are freed for the social cataclysm they have staged to happen. They made it so that even if we try to stop them, we cause it to happen. Once they create their New World Order, they will try to silence those who speak the truth and the Word of God. They worship Lucifer or live by his philosophy. They believe in the world, and those in power want nothing else but to see your soul in hell. If you know the truth, you become a threat, because you can warn others; why not silence the messengers that bring the true Word of God? Most people are ready to follow whatever orders that a civilized world commands of them, even if it means putting innocent people to death. When the world starts to supposedly run out of food, those same people you begged to protect you will chose to do the will of the evil to feed their families. They will follow the commands and laws given to them. Just think about all the stories you heard about the people in Iraq fighting the War on Terrorism and how they slaughtered all those poor people; there is nothing patriotic about that.

THE FALL

Revelation 6:9-11
⁹ And when he had opened the fifth seal, I saw under the altar the souls of them that were slain for the word of God, and for the testimony which they held:

¹⁰ And they cried with a loud voice, saying, How long, O Lord, holy and true, dost thou not judge and avenge our blood on them that dwell on the earth?

¹¹ And white robes were given unto every one of them; and it was said unto them, that they should rest yet for a little season, until their fellowservants also and their brethren, that should be killed as they were, should be fulfilled

The world is full of chaos and we are blind to the fact that what is written in Revelation is happening right now. The sad part about it is, in these times, you rarely hear anything about it in church. The fifth seal caused me to ask myself this: if people were already speaking the word of God and standing up against the evil in this world, why would there even have to be a fifth seal? I mean, a congregation confined to the walls of a church is not good fighting against evil. It's a group of people wanting and searching for a change for the better so that they can exist in an evil world.

When will you choose to stand against everything that is wrong with this world? I believe that once this testimony against them comes out and the Gospel of the Kingdom is preached among all nations, it will cause people to see the truth and speak out against deception. We all have a voice, the people make the difference, and there is strength in numbers. We control our fate and how the rest of this tragic story plays out. What I truly believe is that when people start to notice the deception of what has been going on, they will speak out and some will be imprisoned and some will be killed, as I already stated. Even though you know what is coming, do not run from your destiny; stand together and fight the good fight. They have already begun to notice because of the protesting. People are catching on to their deception and starting to stand up for their rights as human beings and as free people. That's why they just passed a bill that gives them the right to kill and imprison us all. The bill is called the National Defense Authorization Act (NDAA).

Remember when I told you there was a catch to all the good Obama was doing? Well, Obama is the guy everyone loves; you would never expect him to hurt you. He makes you feel safe, he's a great speaker, he has two little girls, he loves his wife, and he sings to the public. You would never suspect him of setting us up. The NDAA bill gives our government the power to kill or imprison anyone anywhere in the world, especially in America, they see as a threat without reason. They can be held without their constitutional right to due process and indefinitely detained without a fair trial for as long as the government wants. So they can't wait for you to fight back. You probably already know the organizations given the power to carry out these acts; you guessed it, the CIA, the military, and if need be, the police. They could throw you away in a concentration camp for as long as they see fit, without reason, maybe even for protesting against what they are doing, especially since the Trespass Bill is working its way through the system and may have already been passed. They already have the concentration camps built all over the United States. They are called FEMA camps, and the government is claiming that they built them because one day they might have to offer aid to another country and bring immigrants to the camps. We all know that's not true; they were designed and built for those who stand against the Illuminati's plan for a one-world government.

The government also gave a company in Georgia a contract to build coffins to put up to three or four people in. They claim it was because of the swine flu spreading in the United States. Whatever it is they're planning, it is going to happen soon, I can feel it. Especially since the bill for FEMA to plan for mass fatality in the U.S. was approved. This bill gives FEMA the power to start preparing funeral homes, cemeteries, and mortuaries just in case they get overwhelmed in the event of a terrorist attack, natural disaster, or other crisis. They are preparing for a war against the people, and the question is, what you are going to do about it?

Some people are so hopelessly dependent on the world we live in that they will even fight to protect it, because it's all they know. If you think you can run and hide from what is coming, think again. You ever heard the phrase "you can run but you can't hide"? They have already started to track and monitor people's location using their cell phones. It's not just the CIA or the FBI, but your local police authorities. They no longer need a warrant to track your cell phone; they can just do it. Not only will they have ground troops, not only will they be able to track you because everything has GPS, not only will they use satellites and camera's, but the FAA is about to start flying 30,000 drone aircrafts, which are used to find terrorists over United States soil. They also have blimps that will float in the air to monitor everything you do on the ground.

If that's not crazy enough, ObamaCare pays for the RFID implant chips that will be mandatory for you to get in the near future. That and the electronic tattoos, which are already FDA approved, called "authentication." Maybe that's why everyone has to pay an extra tax if they don't get it, even if they already have insurance. The 30,000 drones can not only track to see if you have a RFID chip, they can x-ray through your house, just in case you are trying to hide without getting an RFID chip when they become mandatory. Why do you think they convinced you that lead paint was bad for your health? It's because x-rays can't see through lead. The only two choices you have are to either join them or stand against them. I, myself, have chosen to stand against those who are evil. Any president elected, it doesn't matter who we elect as president, is preselected. They all have to carry out the task given to them by the elite. Obama looked like he did some good, but he deals in absolutes, which is a tool of evil. He has put in motion the right bills to track down, enslave, and kill those people who stand against the Illuminati. They will have the weapons, tracking devices, and the numbers, because many people don't know what to believe anymore. They used the deaths of urban youths due to police brutality to transfer the last of the equipment to urban areas. You see, when you protest they just ignore your voices and push their agenda through the media, that sending military equipment to police is needed and justified. As one, we are nothing, but together, we can all make a difference and stand against this evil, but not through violence and rioting.

Bush and Obama used fear to put in place and pass laws, but the question is, were some of those events staged by our government? I believe people can do anything with videos in today's times. You can't believe everything you see or hear on the internet or on TV, but some things that you do see in the media cause you to question what really happened. That's why I want to bring up a few stories that caught my attention, like the Aurora, Colorado, incident and the Sandy Hook shooting. A man named James Holmes ran into a premiere of the new Batman movie and opened fire, wounding 59 people and killing 12. My heart goes out to those victims in the shooting. I just have a few questions and a few things to point out about this story that just don't make a whole lot of sense to me. The very first picture of James Holmes presented before he was seen in court and the picture of James Holmes in court on trial for the murders seem like the same guy at a glance. Then I saw a picture of their faces side by side and they look like two totally different people. The eyes aren't the same, the guy in court has a smaller nose, and the lips are different. Then after the shooter shot into a crowded movie theater, he decided to surrender and warn law enforcement of his booby trapped apartment without being harmed. Then he refused to say anything else. Then everyone in the movie theatre reported multiple gunmen, but reports say only Holmes was there. When they finally get to the gunman's house, they bust out a window and realize that a man who studies neuroscience has created a number of sophisticated bombs in his apartment. Not only just that, but he has buckets of bullets all over the place, all of which he obtained online.

THE FALL

So you're telling me he bought the material to make a bomb, got buckets of bullets, and rush delivered body armor and had it all sent to his apartment? Then, all of a sudden, the gun law the U.N. Arms Trade Treaty, which they tried to pass through that "Fast and Furious" crap finally comes back to the light. Fast and Furious was where the government was selling guns to Mexico, hoping to track the guns to cartel families. They supposedly lost track of the guns and concluded the guns somehow got back into the U.S. after a U.S. border patrol agent was killed. Not only was that a stupid plan, but you try to regulate people having firearms because you messed up. Immediately after this movie theater massacre, the government was talking about pushing this bill through the system and making it a law, but still it wasn't passed.

Then there is the most recent shooting at Sandy Hook Elementary School, where a gunman opened fire and hit 27 people. The majority of the people killed in the elementary shooting where children around the age of six years old. Still, like all the other stories, this story just makes no sense. They chased someone into the woods, and when they caught him, they took him and placed him in the front of the police car. This guy was a possible suspect in the shooting of kids; why put him in the front? Then the ambulances arrived on the scene of the shooting, every last one of them was blocked in, so what was the purpose of them being there? The initial report from the coroner and the police was that the gunman entered the school with an assault rifle, that most of the people were killed with the assault rifle, but there is just one problem with their story: the gunman never took the assault rifle in the building. As a matter of fact, they had no idea the gunman had a rifle in his possession until they found it in his trunk. The police later followed up by saying the gunman used four hand guns. Call me crazy, but doesn't it seem as though the police and the coroner already had their story together, but then once the rifle was found in the trunk by live cameras, they changed up the story? It seems as though they are creating gun violence propaganda to push this gun ban law into existence.

What you need to understand about what is going on is, it isn't just about banning guns, it's about getting you to buy them. They need us to kill each other, especially after they create whatever social cataclysm they are about to create. You see, once chaos breaks out, people will join their ranks to fight for the civilized world they have come to love. That's how you assemble order, gain massive numbers of militarily, and get the population numbers down rapidly. They only have a few more laws to get passed before it's all-out war and they can disarm and massacre thousands, maybe even millions of innocent people. They will throw you into captivity and kill you, but we should not answer with violence. We should answer by keeping the faith, spreading the word, and trying to save as many souls as we can until the end. We should concentrate on making this world free again. Believe in the basics of what Christ has taught us and not what man says we should do. Live the way God intended man to live. Then you will find strength. Then you will not be afraid when the world shall hate you for his name sake. Bush was the start up, Obama was the setup, now who will be the finisher?

> ***Pestilence:*** *a usually fatal epidemic disease, especially bubonic plague (www.thefreedictionary.com/pestilence)*

Throughout history, diseases and plagues have always been a part of life. I haven't really seen evidence of a big plague or disease epidemic that has swept across the globe. However, there has been evidence of plague and disease in certain areas of the world. The first recent case of the bubonic plague in North America popped up in Mexico last year. AIDS is still a worldwide disease and other cases of swine flu, bird flu, Spanish flu, cholera, dengue fever, and a measles outbreak have all appeared in different regions in the world.

I wrote the above part before there was a major outbreak of

Ebola in Africa and now cases of Ebola have started to appear all over the world, including in the United States.

Something else I paid attention to was the fact that the Illuminati may use the world's hunger problems to spread disease. The Monsanto Protection Act protects biotech companies from litigation. The biotech companies deal with genetically engineered seeds and genetically modified organisms. They have been given the go ahead to keep creating these manmade crops and have been granted immunity, basically giving them the right to experiment on us with no consequences in the case that these manmade crops do any harm to anyone. Obama also effectively banned the federal courts from being able to stop the selling or planting of these manmade crops, even if they become a health risk. Those genetic crops made me think about the bees; could they be dying off from trying to pollinate modified crops? One of the biggest reasons I believe the government is planning on releasing a plague or disease in the near future is because of the endless fields of coffins they are making. I mean, what are all those coffins for, what are they planning, and who will be in them? All of this reminds me of the murals in the Denver airport. Check them out. Not only is there a pale horseman statue, but they also painted how we will die. One little girl in one of the FEMA coffins is even holding a Bible.

I also wonder if they are planning to release some type of plague or disease with these Chemtrails that we see sweeping the sky. Also, could chemtrails be the reason for the deaths of all those animals across the globe? Since New Year's Eve of 2010, there have been massive animal deaths across the world, and experts really have no real answer for the deaths.

> **Hosea 4:2–3**
> *² By swearing, and lying, and killing, and stealing, and committing adultery, they break out, and blood toucheth blood.*
> *³ Therefore shall the land mourn, and every one that dwelleth therein shall languish, with the beasts of the field,*

and with the fowls of the heaven; yea, the fishes of the sea also shall be taken away.

100,000 drum fish dead Arkansas River/5,000 red winged black birds Beebe, Arkansas/100 tons of fish Brazilian Coast/starling, red winged black birds, sparrows Pointe Coupee Parish, Louisiana/2 million dead fish Chesapeake Bay, Maryland/8,000 dead turtle doves in Faenza, Italy, and Kentucky/hundreds of birds on a California highway/ thousands of dead gizzard shad off the harbors of Chicago/ 200 cows dead in Stockton, Wisconsin/ 40,000 dead crabs in England/ 7,000 dead Buffalo in Vietnam/hundreds of dead seals in Canada/4,000 dead birds in Guanajuato, Mexico/877 dolphins in Peru/538 pelicans in Peru (www. end-times-prophecy.org/animals-deaths)

They still can't explain what happened to all of those animals across the world. I'm wondering if the chemicals that are being released into earth's atmosphere are having side effects on the agricultural and ecological system. Every day more and more massive animal deaths are occurring around the world, and nobody is saying anything about it. I really don't know all the side effects of chemtrails, but here is what I do know through researching these mysterious lines in the sky across the world.

If you're wondering and don't know what chemtrails are, then let me explain. Have you ever just walked outside looked up into the sky and seen a streak or a spider web that looks like a plane was dragging a cloud behind it? Then you look around in every direction and there isn't a plane in sight. When I was young, I used to think it was some type of air show going on and I had missed it, but now I know that the lines left behind are more than just exhaust from the jets crossing the sky. I believe they were chemtrails, chemicals that are released into the atmosphere by the government. The government denies chemtrails and the spilling of chemicals out of aerosol containers into are atmosphere. A real jet's exhaust takes seconds to disappear out of the sky. Chemtrails takes hours and sometimes as long as a day. I have even caught one of the planes running out of whatever it was releasing. When it was done, the jet exhaust turned regular, and it stopped spilling chemicals into the air. Could the government be getting prepared for chemical or biological warfare? They're doing it all over the world, claiming the release of aluminum into the atmosphere is to block harmful radiation from the sun and to cool the earth from global warming.

Some theories of the mysterious chemtrails are that it could be used for depopulation. After all, breathing in enough aluminum vapors could cause side effects like respiratory problems, and soft metals have also been linked to making people mentally insane. Maybe that's why all my life I have never had allergies then I just grew into them. Another theory is that the reason for the aerosol program is to geo-engineer the climate and the weather. They say that it is a program to stop global warming, but their idea for releasing chemicals in the air for global warming sounds a lot like the concept for engineering the climate and weather. These chemtrails that are being released form a dense layer of artificial cloud cover, affecting weather radars. Many believe this weapon of mass destruction could be used to cause floods, droughts, hurricanes, and earthquakes. I believe the government can activate these atmospheric disturbances at will and that they have been doing it for years.

There have been all types of earthquakes of different magnitudes devastating countries around the world. They have increased over time and the death toll is rising every year. The following are some earthquakes that happened around the world, just to name a few, through the years.

- On March 11, 2011, an 8.9 magnitude earthquake devastated the people of Japan. The earthquake was centered off the northeast coast of Honshu, Japan. It unleashed a tsunami wave into Japan that destroyed everything in its path.

- On February 21, 2011, a 6.3 magnitude earthquake hit the

South Island in New Zealand and its largest city of Christ Church. The earthquake claimed the lives of 181 people. Seismologists say that it was due to a new fault line they were unaware of in the earth's crust.

- On Tuesday, January 12, 2010, a 7.0 magnitude earthquake shook the people of Haiti. The earthquake affected over 3 million people and left over a million people homeless and without food, water, and aid. The earthquake left homes and businesses severely damaged and some of them had collapsed. By January 24th, at least 52 aftershocks measuring 4.5 or greater had been recorded.

- On May 12, 2008, a 7.9 magnitude earthquake struck the people on Sichuan, China. An estimated 90,000 people were either killed or missing and it was the country's worst earthquake in decades.

- On August 15, 2007, an 8.0 magnitude earthquake struck Pisco, Peru, destroying 80% of the homes. An estimated 500 people were killed and thousands were left homeless.

- On October 8, 2005, a 7.6 magnitude earthquake hit Kashmir, Pakistan. It claimed the lives of at least 86,000 people and more than 69,000 were injured in the quake.

- On December 26, 2004, a 9.1 magnitude earthquake devastated the island of Sumatra in Indonesia. The quake caused a Tsunami claiming over 200,000 lives. It left an estimated 1.7 million people displaced across the Pacific Region.

- On December 26, 2003, a 6.6 magnitude earthquake hit Bam, Iran. This earthquake that hit the ancient city of Bam claimed the lives of an estimated 31,000 people.

(www.nbcnews.com)

THE FALL

Natural disasters, such as tsunamis, hurricanes, tornadoes, and earthquakes, have always been a part of life. These natural disasters are dangerous and have increased in numbers and taken many lives over the years. They have also hit places in the world that normally don't have earthquakes. Many scientists believe that the increase in natural disasters may be because the earth's poles are shifting at an alarming rate. I used to believe that could be the only cause, until I researched HAARP, a facility located in Alaska. HAARP stands for High Frequency Active Auroral Research Program and they're also the people who control chemtrails. The idea for this program came from Nikola Tesla, a mechanical and electrical engineer, who many believed to be a mad scientist. Thomas Edison and his assistant even believed that Nikola could hear and speak to spirits. Among other inventions, he came up with the idea of a particle beam weapon and a death ray. Dr. Bernard Eastlund patented plans for how an electromagnetic wave generator could be built and used. Dr. Eastlund became an employee of HAARP and helped with the development of this weapon of mass destruction that the government claims is strictly in the name of research. Since when has the government done research on anything and not used it as a weapon? They're using very large antennas that utilize large amounts of power to beam radio waves up into the ionosphere. Some scientists believe that when you heat up the ionosphere with the right amount of watts, you can cause geophysical events. I'm a CNC programmer and machinist, and I happen to know that aluminum is cheap, lightweight, and heats up very fast, which is probably why they're spilling it into the atmosphere, along with other chemicals. I believe HAARP has the technology that can cause artificial earthquakes, volcanic eruptions, and tsunamis; they can engineer the weather, and if beamed in the right direction, it could shut down global communication and create blackouts in areas. I believe HAARP could also be responsible for all the sink holes appearing around the world today. Which makes me ask the questions about whether it is man or Mother Nature who has claimed the lives of so many people over the years.

In 2003 there was a blackout in the northeast, which was the second most wide-spread blackout in history. It affected people in Ontario, Canada, and in eight U.S. states, including the place I live, Michigan. It was said that Canada blamed a power plant in New York, saying lightning struck the plant, causing the failure. New York responded by saying that the power plant that was rumored to be struck by lightning was still fully operational at the time and that there was no rainstorm around the time that all the power went out. Canada responded by saying there must have been an outage at a nuclear plant in Pennsylvania. State authorities for Pennsylvania responded by saying all the plants were functioning normally and that, in fact, was not the cause of the blackout. I have been looking for who to blame or what really caused the overload. Any way it goes, I believe the blackout happened on purpose, and HAARP could very well have been behind it. I believe it was a test to see what we would do if we had no power. How would we react knowing that all the power was out everywhere and how long it would take to restore power after it was lost.

When the blackout first happened, I remember going to the store to get enough to drink for a couple of days. While I was waiting to pay, I noticed everyone was just snatching stuff and leaving. One of the guys was dancing on the way out the store with a 24-pack of beer. The owners were too scared to come from behind the counter to stop them from stealing. There were too many people in there trying to buy supplies, and with no power, that meant no cameras; anything could have happened. You could see the fear in the store owners' eyes as they watched people take advantage of the power failure. All that happened within the first couple of hours of the blackout. The real danger started when people realized it might be a few days before it came back on. People started sleeping during the day and staying awake during the night, fearing that people were going to come into their houses while they were sleeping. The day after the blackout happened, the only thing I kept hearing was what got robbed or what they were going to hit next. I had never seen so many people praying that the power would come back on in my life, not only because of the summer heat, not because they were running out of food and water, but because they feared for their lives. It never got as bad as I thought it would get, but then again, the lights were only out a few days before power was restored. I asked myself, was this some type of government test to see what we would do if we had no computers, lights, television, air conditioning, got low on food and water, and had no one to call for help? I started thinking to myself, was it a test the government forced on us or was this electrical power outage caused by some other natural, catastrophic event? I wondered, is this what it is going to look like when the world ends? Also, if that was only a few days, then what would it have looked like after a few weeks, or even worse, months? Then the thought of what HAARP is capable of made me start to look at the Katrina disaster, wondering if that could have also been some type of government test.

On August 25, 2005, Hurricane Katrina hit land as a Category 1 hurricane in Florida, destroying everything in its path. Unexpectedly, Hurricane Katrina took a hard left and passed straight through the Gulf of Mexico, where it became a Category 5 hurricane. The hurricane weakened to a Category 3 hurricane, but it still would be deadly. Then it made its second touchdown on the border of Mississippi and Louisiana. Katrina was the worst natural disaster the United States has ever seen. Katrina caused a large part of the state of Louisiana to flood and left parts of it covered in water, some parts under 15 feet in water maybe more. Most of the levees designed by the United States Army Corps of Engineers broke. The system of levees was a complete failure and some would say one of the worst engineering disasters in history. The breaches and the failure of the flood walls because of the broken levees was the main thing responsible for most of the flooding in those areas under water. Most people left in New Orleans after the hurricane hit took refuge in the Superdome, and others swam for their lives or remained in attics or on rooftops until help arrived. The flooding caused oil refineries to shut down, which drove the prices of oil up, sending gas prices up yet again. Tens of thousands of troops and volunteers came together to try to save lives and rescue the survivors. Many survived, but because so many of the deceased were floating in the water, many people walking in the water contracted diseases.

The biggest problem with what happened after Katrina is the fact that it took FEMA three days to respond and get water, food, medical supplies, and other aid to the Superdome and the survivors of this devastating natural disaster. At least that's what they said, but we know it was more like five days to get supplies to the survivors. Then FEMA claims to have had no knowledge of the 2,000 survivors in the convention center and took even longer to get them relief. People in politics said America just wasn't ready for this type of natural disaster. We know that's not true, because we are ready within a day to aid other countries in times of natural disasters, but when it hits home, we don't know what to do. The American Red Cross even tried to get into New Orleans to pass out food to survivors, but because the military was supposedly saving lives in search and rescues, they were asked to wait. That fact also made me upset, because isn't passing out food part of saving lives too? I mean, that food could have saved even more lives, especially for the people with medical conditions.

After the U.S. Senate passed a relief package bill, the next day President Bush signed the $10.5 billion relief package. They evacuated all the survivors in the Superdome and the rest of the survivors. Nobody knows why it took so long for them to get those people some relief, but some people took it as President Bush was a racist and hated black people. I hope that wasn't the case, and I don't think it was; I just think it was the perfect setting for the government's project. On top of all that, they started putting the survivors from Hurricane Katrina in hazardous toxic trailers. I believe that the government did all of it to see how people would react when everything was taken away from them. How would people react when they didn't have food, water, and supplies? How would people react when they had nobody to call for help? My friend who was a survivor that moved up here after Katrina hit was in the Dome. He told me all of the things that happened in the Dome and how people reacted to not having anything. All I kept thinking about was, what if one day it was the whole world without food, water, and supplies? What would we do then, fight for survival or fight each other; would we kill for a loaf of bread? Those in power know that after a catastrophic event or worldwide economical failure, most people will have to turn to them. Then they will have absolute power over the world.

Picture the Holocaust, but this time it's the whole world. Now picture the people hunting you down are people from your family and your friends, because they are hungry and chose the other side. How far would people go to provide for their families? Would they take the mark of the beast to feed their families? I believe that a lot of people can say what they won't do until they get pushed into a bad situation. People nowadays, when they're pushed into a world of chaos and are scared, they look for the person with the easiest and quickest solution, especially when that person presents himself as the good guy. That's what the Illuminati means when they say "order out of chaos," because they're referring to the easily influenced mind when people are scared. What big event will cause chaos on earth and drive people into a total state of fear, along with what has already happened? I believe the disasters that could give them the power they need to control the world could be World War III, a global economic collapse, a global attack by HAARP, solar flares, or any major global natural disaster. World War III could start any day now, but we are already fighting a war against those who have tried to enslave our minds. Soon they will try to completely rule the world in a one-world government. My question to you is, will you join them, or will you become freed from slavery and fight for your freedom and every God-given right we are all born with? Will you speak out the Gospel of the Kingdom, which is the truth, or will you continue to live in deception and teach lies? Do you still believe in everything that's righteous and of the Father or do you believe in everything this world has taught you? Can you honestly say your heart is filled with love or is it saturated with hate? I believe God is humbling me, teaching me, and getting me prepared for The War. The last war, us versus them, the fight against good and evil. The choice is yours. What will you choose, slavery or freedom?

CHAPTER 11

THE WRATH OF GOD

After all the chaos and the time of purification, the time where people begin to understand and see the truth, according to the book of Matthew, after the rise of the antichrist and the false prophet, the next thing that will happen is the opening of the sixth seal. There are many scriptures describing this event, and all of those scriptures make me think about why the Bible says blessed is he that waits until the three and a half years after the antichrist comes to power. I believe that after three and a half years, God, himself, may send the Son of Man and angels to intervene with what's happening on earth, but before intervening, they seal the heads of his people so that they aren't harmed during the wrath.

> ***Revelation 6:12–17***
>
> [12] *And behold when he opened the sixth seal, and, lo, there was a great earthquake; and the sun became black as sackcloth of hair, and the moon became as blood;*
>
> [13] *And the stars of heaven fell unto the earth, even as a fig tree casteth her untimely figs, when she is shaken of the mighty wind.*
>
> [14] *And the heaven departed as a scroll when it is rolled together; and every mountain and island were moved out of there place*

> ¹⁵ *And the kings of the earth, and the great men, and the rich men, and the chief captains, and the mighty men, and every bondman, and every free man, hid themselves in the dens and in the rocks of the mountains;*
> ¹⁶ *And said to the mountains and rocks, Fall on us, and hide us from the face of him that sitteth on the throne, and from the wrath of the Lamb:*
> ¹⁷ *For the great day of his wrath is come; and who shall be able to stand?*

The Anunnaki claimed to have been from a planet called Nibiru. It is through the study of the Sumerians that scientists also started to look for Planet X. The Sumerians left behind an artifact showing our solar system, but in their map, they had an extra planet. NASA has made numerous reports of finding something that seems to be another planet moving in space using infrared readings. On January 30, 1983, John Noble Wilford printed an article in *The New York Times* with the title "Clues Get Warm in the Search for Planet X." The article claimed that gravitational forces were tugging at Uranus and Neptune, causing irregularities in there orbits. It made scientists begin to renew the search for this tenth planet in our solar system. Then, on December 30, 1983, Thomas O'Toole published in the *Washington Post* that they had found something possibly as large as Jupiter in space, calling it a mysterious heavenly body that was so close to earth it could be in this solar system. Scientist couldn't tell if it was a giant comet, a planet, or a "protostar" that never got hot enough to become a star. Even just recently, in 2011, it was reported on CNN that a large, hidden heavenly body was in fact in our solar system.

I believe it is an approaching planet, because the same thing that happened to Uranus and Neptune is what I believe is now happening to planet earth, but it is hard to tell, because the Milky Way also has a strong gravitational pull. Maybe that is why scientists are recording that the earth is wobbling. I'm no expert, but I do know a little bit about magnets, and if the earth's magnetic field is being pulled and twisted by a force, it might be because there is something else out there with a massive magnetic field. All I know is NASA has begun to shut down its main satellites and its space program, claiming it is because of a lack of funding. That alone makes me think they're hiding something.

I asked myself, how did an ancient civilization know all the planets in our solar system and why was there an extra planet? Did they have some type of device or powerful telescope that allowed them to see into space or have space travel? I don't believe they did, but I believe it's possible. Some believe ancient civilizations were very technologically advanced, but I have not seen any real evidence that suggests they had the technology to see as far into space as we can today. So I asked myself, how did they know about all of the planets in the solar system? I believe that their pagan gods gave them the knowledge of space and time. It was the Mayans who became obsessed with time and the alignment of the planets. Some experts believe the earth's poles have been caused to shift at an alarming rate. I believe it's because a force that could possibly be a planet with an enormous gravitational pull is approaching. The theories on Nibiru suggest that the planet maybe eight times the size of earth and that it moves so slowly that we only ever see it every 3,600 years. Some scientist even believe it may be what killed the dinosaurs and destroyed prehistoric life on this planet. Nibiru moves through our solar system on a path like a comet in an elliptical orbit. If this planet does exist and is returning, some astrologists believe it will pass in-between the earth and the sun. In the Bible, the sixth seal describes a cosmic occurrence that will happen in space and will have a deadly effect on earth. Venus isn't big enough to block the sun and turn the moon red as blood. If something eight times the size of earth did pass in-between earth and the sun, it could cause an eclipse, making the sun look black.

Many believe planet Nibiru could be a red planet, so if the sun's reflection hits off of Nibiru, it could make the moon look as red as blood. If Nibiru hits another planet or has a gravitational pull strong enough to attract rocks to it, rocks could be floating around it or trailing the massive planet. If some of those rocks were to stray off and hit earth, it would look as though stars were falling from the sky. The great earthquake would be caused by the shifting of the earth, and everything on earth would be out of place because of the pole shift. Some scientists believe that the North Pole would end up somewhere near the equator. The gravitational pull would cause the tides to rise and the wind to become intense. Just think about how the tides rise when the moon gets too close to earth. If this planet does exist, and I believe it does, within a few years, we should be able to see it clearly. Even though I believe some have seen it already in the last few years, because there have been a lot of news reports of two suns in the sky. We cannot see the planet clearly; that is why I believe that it cannot possibly be here by the end of this year. Whenever it comes, we will see it before it gets here, because like the Bible says it will be panic and fear. It also says people will have time to hide in the dens and the mountains. I believe no matter how much they want to hide it, how many satellites and programs the government shuts down, they can't keep it a secret for too long.

> **Luke 21:25–26**
> *25 And there shall be signs in the sun, and in the moon, and in the stars, and upon the earth distress of nations, with perplexity; the sea and the waves roaring;*
> *26 Men's hearts failing them for fear, and for looking after those things which are coming on the earth: for the powers of heaven shall be shaken.*

This thought of another planet and this scripture made me ask myself, what is heaven? I mean, if God created the heavens and the earth, heaven wouldn't just be some place in the clouds. What if heaven is an actual planet? If when these events happen man says to hide from him who is on the throne, man has to know God is there, not an act of science or bad luck. His wrath upon the earth

THE WRATH OF GOD

for all that man has done. Before the sixth seal is unleashed, God will speak to his angels and tell them to stop until they have sealed the foreheads of his servants who spoke the word of God, who kept the faith and were obedient unto him and did not receive the mark. Who were not deceived by lies, but stood up, spoke the truth, and were righteous. Those people will be protected during God's wrath.

Revelation 7:3

³ Saying, Hurt not the earth, neither the sea, nor the trees, till we have sealed the servants of our God in their foreheads.

After the foreheads of the righteous were sealed they were praised up in heaven.

They are gathered from all the corners of the earth, and as those 144,000 of the Jewish tribes are taken away and called up, God also calls up a large number of righteous who are not of the Jewish tribes. Those are the Gentiles that chose God during these troubled times we live in and chose not to live wickedly and repented for their sins. The number of Gentiles is so many people that no man could count how many people there were and they will be dressed in white robes.

Revelation 7:9–16

⁹ After this I beheld, and, lo, a great multitude, which no man could number, of all nations, and kindreds, and people, and tongues, stood before the Lamb, clothed with white robes, and palms in their hands;

¹⁰ And cried with a loud voice, saying, Salvation to our God which sitteth upon the throne, and unto the Lamb.

¹¹ And all the angels stood round about the throne, and about the elders and the four beasts, and fell before the throne on their faces, and worshipped God,

¹² Saying, Amen: Blessing, and glory, and wisdom, and

> *thanksgiving, and honour, and power, and might, be unto our God for ever and ever. Amen.*
>
> *[13] And one of the elders answered, saying unto me, What are these which are arrayed in white robes? And whence came they?*
>
> *[14] And I said unto him, Sir, thou knowest. And he said to me, These are they which came out of great tribulation, and have washed their robes, and make them white in the blood of the Lamb.*
>
> *[15] Therefore are they before the throne of God, and serve him day and night in his temple: and he that sitteth on the throne shall dwell among them.*
>
> *[16] They shall hunger no more, neither thirst any more; neither shall the sun light on them, nor any heat.*

The seven seals are signs that the end is near and that Christ is on his way back to deliver his people from all the evil in this world. God is displeased with the world; we have abandoned and we have forgotten his commandments. We no longer know ourselves and have been deceived and persuaded by evil. Most people don't want to change and repent for their sins, because they are slaves to this world. We are living in a world where we sin on a daily basis and it is viewed as the right thing to do. We are comfortable with breaking the commandments and doing evil when we should hate sin. We are living in a world where love and compassion for each other is barely shown. Christ is displeased with us, even in the churches. We should all repent for our sins and try to change in Christ, our first love, because no man wants to be here during the seventh seal. After the sixth seal, God gives his angels the power to carry out destruction on earth.

Revelation 8:1–5

> *[1] And when he had opened the seventh seal, there was silence in heaven about the space of half an hour.*

> *² And I saw the seven angels which stood before God; and to the were given seven trumpets.*
> *³ And another angel came and stood at the altar, having a golden censer; and there was given unto him much incense, that he should offer it with the prayers of all saints upon the golden altar which was before the throne.*
> *⁴ And the smoke of the incense, which came with the prayers of the saints, ascended up before God out of the angel's hand.*
> *⁵ And the angel took the censer, and filled it with fire of the altar, and cast it into the earth: and there were voices, and thunderings, and lightnings, and an earthquake.*

The trumpets are plagues and catastrophes that happen to the earth. I believe the things that happen are an aftershock of the sixth seal and the earth may be hit by the rocks trailing Planet X. During the first four trumpets, a third of crops, trees, and green life will be destroyed. A large amount of the oceans, seas, and rivers will be poisoned. The life in these bodies of water will become dead and the water will become blood. Those who are left here after the seals will be faced with a difficult choice, because those in power who serve evil know people's weaknesses and that they will be tempted with the most basic of things. God promises that he shall keep his people from the hour of temptation, but those left behind will be tempted the same way Lucifer tempted Christ when he was fasting for forty days and forty nights. During that time they will be the only people that will have the things you need to survive. As I've said, governments all around the world have been building bunkers and stockpiling food, water, and supplies. They are rapidly preparing for something, and we should be to, whether it be preparing for change or the survival of earth's destruction. At first when the economy fails, or whatever social cataclysm they create, they will offer food and water to look like the savior. After giving to the helpless and getting everyone to trust them, they will demand that you pledge your allegiance to them. They will offer you and your family security against a world in chaos. It is the second beast, the false prophet, that gives the antichrist the power to tempt the world.

> **Revelations 13:15–17**
> ¹⁵ And he had power to give life unto the image of the beast, that the image of the beast should both speak, and cause that as many as would not worship the image of the beast should be killed.
> ¹⁶ And he causeth all, both small and great, rich and poor, free and bond, to receive a mark in their right hand, or in their forehead
> ¹⁷ And that no man might buy or sell, save he that had the mark, or the name of the beast, or the number of his name.

They have been preparing the world to go to a cashless society for years. Credit cards, bank cards, buying online, paying bills with your smart phones are all ways we buy or pay bills without actually using paper money. Preparing you for a future of not needing money and being able to buy things with the RFID chips they implant in you. That's why they promote getting direct deposit, saying it saves paper, but then still send the stub with a voided check; it's the same amount of paper, right? They are promoting people not using paper money as much in today's times to make the transition to a cashless society.

I fear people will be left with a very hard decision and will be tempted in ways unimaginable. It is one thing for you to be hungry and thirsty, but when you have to watch the people you love starve to death or die from dehydration, that is a whole other thing. If we can't change, I would say, "Stay strong," to those people who have to wait here on earth until Christ returns. Be faithful, even if it leads to your death, and pray always. Do not believe anyone that says they are the Messiah or Christ, for they will do great miracles, but when Christ returns, everyone will know. Do not be tempted and except the mark of the beast.

When the fifth trumpet is sounded, I believe Satan will be

unleashed from the bottomless pit and will gain power over the world. In ancient times, Satan had to travel; he deceived man and was worshipped by different people in different time periods. Now all he has to do is perform a couple of miracles on TV and the Internet then he is worshipped by everyone in the world. It won't be hard to do. Some people believe in religious leaders already that claim to do miracles. They claim to have the power to heal and they touch people on the head, shake a little bit, people fake faint, and instantly, they're healed. I believe in the power of healing through Christ, but I also believe some men that claim to be of God are frauds, and most people can't tell the difference. Some people don't know what to believe because of their hardships in life. I believe some people will believe in anything, because most people just need something or someone to believe in. They want to believe in something so bad they don't care if it's good or evil, as long as it sounds good to a civilized world. In a world of chaos, they will probably be easily influenced by a man that does miracles. Some people believe in and are already awaiting the false messiah's arrival in the Middle East. Keep your faith through all your trials you face in life, even when it seems all hope is lost. The Bible says we should hate sin and love Christ. We all have a light that shines in us and that is the key to our salvation.

> **Matthew 5:14–16**
>
> [14] Ye are the light of the world. A city that is set on an hill cannot be hid.
>
> [15] Neither do men light a candle, and put it under bushel, but on a candlestick; and it giveth light unto all that are in the house.
>
> [16] Let your light so shine before men, that they may see your good works, and glorify your Father which is in heaven.

If you are truly someone of God, you will let that light of truth shine and you will try to warn the world about the darkness and deception that now rules the world. When the New World Order comes to pass, the world will be completely dominated by evil. The people left here after the seven seals are those people who God says are in-between or wicked. If you still don't choose to put your faith in God after all the signs you see, and you are not strong in Christ, and you have little faith, I will pray for you. I fear during these times you will be tempted in ways unimaginable. You may think we have it rough now, but this is nothing compared to what's coming. The antichrist, false prophet, and Lucifer are about to take control of this world. If we cannot change, only the people who seek Christ and keep their faith in these last days will be saved. Stop trying to rationalize and convince yourself that the wrong things you may be doing are right; stop being afraid to change. They have lied and kept you in the dark your whole life. Those people who feel like they can't change because this life of doing wrong is the only thing they've ever known, remember that all things are possible through Christ, because the life we are living is a life of sin and he is waiting to deliver you.

> **Philippians 4:13**
>
> [13] *I can do all things through Christ which strengtheneth me.*

We will never be perfect, but we can choose God, change our lives, and change the world. I believe that through change we can stop the seven seals from being broken, and if not, God, let your will be done. Through God we can start to love each other, and through him we can stand against the evil in this world together. We can finally liberate ourselves from slavery and finally be free. I can't do this task alone, but together we can all repent for our sins and show God that we have the ability to change. We can take away the power that Lucifer has over our minds and the power those in control have over the people. We can move closer to being in God's grace and living the way he has always intended mankind to live. If we can change as a whole, begin to love each other, and stay faithful to the word of God, we can prevent the seals from all being broken. We can show God that we see his warnings and we have the ability to change. Lucifer will have no power here, and it would be pointless for him to return. That would mean repenting and living your life free of worldly ways.

We must first teach ourselves to survive, live by the true word, and devote ourselves to doing what's right. Going back to times where you were happy with the simple things in life and not depending on corporations, banks, and systems for everything. I'm talking about a time when we were equal, free, and believed in helping each other, a time when we were dependent on ourselves for survival, without the influence of others. A time without hatred; people only hate one another because that's what the world has manipulated us and taught us to do; it was learned. You were not born that way. We fear what we don't understand. Racism exists only to keep us separated, because divided we are conquered and controlled. Most of the world has been conquered mentally, spiritually, and physically, but we can choose to take our lives back. We can seek refuge in the Lord, for he will come and save us from the darkness that has covered the world.

I always hear people use the phrase "God knows my heart" when referring to religion and their lives. They use it as an excuse to do evil or to explain the evil they have done. I believe God can see and knows what's in your heart, but I believe the world needs to see it a little bit more. Christ says there are three types of people: those that are saved and serve God, those that do evil, and those that are in-between. Which of these are you, because the people in-between will be judged, and a lot of them will be on earth in those days of temptation. Most people believe that everything they are doing is right, but with the seven seals being broken, I am guessing that the lives most of us live aren't in the service of God, that this world is full of people who do evil and are in-between. Most of the in-between people want to change, but some of them are afraid. They are afraid to leave the only life they've ever known behind. They are afraid of what people will think of them. That they won't be accepted by society, by their friends, or by loved ones. They're afraid that people will look at them funny for being nice, compassionate, kindhearted, and loving. Some people are afraid that when they go to Christ, they'll be broke, because they can't hustle anymore. They don't know or understand that the true richest are in Christ and that he will provide us with everything we need. Those people have little faith in the power of God and what he can do for a person's life. They are afraid that when they go to Christ, the fun stops and life will somehow get boring.

If people find joy in doing evil and sinning, then they really don't know the joys and peace of being saved in Christ. They're afraid of letting that light that shines inside of everyone shine bright on the world. They're afraid of forgiving their enemies, those people that do wrong against them or hate them. I know because I have been there and I am overcoming my foolish ways. I had to ask myself, was the life I was living really worth me going to hell? I lost some of my friends when I started to change my life, but by me setting an example, my friends slowly began changing their lives too. We can all choose to change for the better, and I believe that what is happening can be stopped. It is up to us to choose to repent for our sins. We have the power to stop the upcoming war and any other evil that stands against us by speaking out and showing the world love and truth.

> **Martin Luther King, Jr.**
> *Darkness cannot drive out darkness; only light can do that. Hate cannot drive out hate; only love can do that. (http://www.goodreads.com/quotes/943-darkness-cannot-drive-out-darkness-only-light-can-do-that)*

We can take away the influence that Lucifer and the fallen angels have on this earth. Think about if this Planet X does exist and it's on the path of a comet. That would mean it's impossible to predict its path through our solar system. What if we can change and the wrath of God passes us by and we can stop the sixth seal from being broken? The time to stand is now, as we enter the fifth seal and overcome the evil of this world. If the sixth seal is broken, we shouldn't hide in the mountains; instead, we should pray and repent for our sins. If we can't change and the seven seals are broken, life still goes on, and Christ is still not going to return, but then again, I shouldn't say that, because no man knows the date and time of his return. We can only see the warnings he told us to be watchful of in the end.

Many would try to convince you that the rapture happens first, that the children of God will not see the world in such chaos. Well, newsflash, we are living in such times. Many men of faith just believe what they have been taught and don't do the research themselves. John Nelson Darby was the man who created the dispensation on the end times, Bible prophecies, and the Rapture that most churches believe today. I believe the only reason he created it was so while the Illuminati is completing its goal, we would look at the world in a state of denial and not believe. So that you wouldn't do the main thing Christ tells us to do during these troubled times, and that is remaining watchful.

> **Arthur W. Pink**
> *Dispensationalism is a device of the enemy, designed to rob the children of no small part of that bread which their heavenly father has provided for their souls a device in wherein the wily serpent appears as an angel of light, feigning to "make the Bible a new book" by simplifying much in it which perplexes the spiritually unlearned. It is sad to see how widely successful the devil has been by means of this subtle innovation. (http:regal-network.com/dispensationalism/)*

After John Darby created dispensation, many churches took on the belief and started teaching it, and they have continued to teach his theory to this day. Many people wrote about John Darby during his time, and even he, himself, had many writings. It is because of those writings many believed that he was also a Freemason. Many believe he belonged to a lodge that was believed to have taught cabalism. Meaning, even though he is known as the father of dispensation and the father of the Rapture doctrine, and he was perceived to be a minister of God, he may have also practiced magic, sorcery, and witchcraft. If he was a Freemason, he would have been one around the same time members of the Illuminati joined the Freemasons, and their goal was to conquer, control, infiltrate, and influence all government and religion. John also helped to form a religious group known as the Plymouth Brethren, a group who many, including myself, believe was and is an occult organization because of its practices. Aleister Crowley, a man who practiced magic, was a known Luciferian, a drug abuser, a bi-sexual occultist, and known in his day as "the wickedest man in the world." He was raised within the Exclusive Brethren, which is a part of the Plymouth Brethren. In his memoirs, he considered the Brethren's teachings and practices as essential for understanding his views.

George Müeller
My brother, I am a constant reader of my Bible, and I soon found that what I was taught to believe did not always agree with what my Bible said. I came to see that I must either part company with John Darby, or my precious Bible, and I chose to cling to my Bible and part from Mr. Darby. (http:regal-network.com/dispensationalism/)

No matter what type of person he was, whether he was inspired by good or evil, Darby could not have possibly known what was going to happen, unless he was helping to plan it. I believe his theory and his interpretation of the Rapture coming before the seven seals is wrong. In the end, Daniel said that the wise would understand. Which means to me very few people would see the truth until the Gospel of the Kingdom is spoken throughout the world.

The true Gospel of Christ is written in the hearts of all mankind through love and in the goodness in life. If your religion causes you to not believe in Christ, you would have to agree that in order to have such an influential impact on the world, he must have been an exceptional man. When I learned that ancient civilizations believed everybody had to go to the underworld, and that the reason we don't have to go to the underworld with sinister gods is because Christ died for our sins. That right there makes me believe in him so much more. We all make mistakes and are guilty of committing sin, but do you learn from your mistakes, is your heart free to love, and do you hate the sins you have committed and work to be better as a person in Christ in a world designed and influenced by Lucifer to do evil? Start working together and doing for others more than you do for yourself. Christ believes in you, loves you, and blessed is the day that you realize you need nothing of this world but to except him into your life. This is what I believe, nothing more, and hopefully, my thoughts in this book will open and touch your heart as it has touched mine.

The time is now for people to rise up and speak with the swords of their mouth about the deception Satan has left on earth. To guide the lost into the arms of Christ and stand against those who are wicked. Pray for me as I will pray for you. All those who know the truth hear his voice. This world was built for mankind to live on in peace, free and with love for one another. We live in this sinful world where we live as slaves, and we believe the only way we will ever be able to live free again is by making it through the gates of heaven. We don't realize this world was meant to be a paradise and a kingdom and that we can choose to make this place a paradise again. We have lost our way and this place is no longer a kingdom. The word gospel means the good news. So the Gospel of the Kingdom is that once you realize the truth about history and the deception of the fallen, when you realize all of this was an organized plan from the beginning, then you will realize why the world is the way it is today. You will realize what is of God and what is not, what God wanted from us from the beginning, and what Christ was really trying to teach.

1 John 2:24-27

²⁴ Let that therefore abide in you, which ye have heard from the beginning. If that which ye have heard from the beginning shall remain in you, ye also shall continue in the Son, and in the Father

²⁵ And this is the promise that he hath promised us, even eternal life.

²⁶ These things have I written unto you concerning them that seduce you.

²⁷ But the anointing which ye have received of him abideth in you, and ye need not that any man teach you: but as the same anointing teacheth you of all things, and is truth, and is no lie, and even as it hath taught you, ye shall abide in him.

You will understand that we need nothing of this world but to except him, and that it is you who has a direct connection to God, Christ, and the Holy Spirit. You will begin to know yourself, who you are and why you act the way you do. We can truly worship God in spirit and in truth. I believe by exposing the deception of the fallen, understanding the truth that is God, and beginning to truly know ourselves, we can set ourselves free from the traps that have been placed before us and that have imprisoned and seduced our minds all our lives. Then we will find the Kingdom of God, inside of us and all around us. Then you will know God and have the strength to stand against the evil that has overcome the world we know today. No matter how you look at the world, whether it is from a religious or a scientific point of view, you will see that the world as we know it is coming to an end. I leave you with the scripture my mother used to read to me every day before I went to school. It comes from the book of Ephesians, and when reading it, I realized the scripture she had been reading to me all my life was preparing me to stand at this very moment.

Ephesians 6:10–13

[10] Finally, my brethren, be strong in the Lord, and in the power of his might.

[11] Put on the whole armour of God, that ye may be able to stand against the wiles of the devil.

[12] For we wrestle not against flesh and blood, but against principalities, against powers, against spiritual wickedness in high places.

[13] Wherefore take unto you the whole armour of God, that ye may be able to withstand in the evil days, and having done all, to stand.

CPSIA information can be obtained
at www.ICGtesting.com
Printed in the USA
FFOW04n0057081215
19227FF